HAUNTED
TUNBRIDGE
WELLS

HAUNTED
TUNBRIDGE
WELLS

Neil Arnold

The
History
Press

This book is dedicated, with love, to Susie, Bob, Charlotte and Sam

First published 2013

The History Press
The Mill, Brimscombe Port
Stroud, Gloucestershire, GL5 2QG
www.thehistorypress.co.uk

British Library Cataloguing in Publication Data.
A catalogue record for this book is available from the British Library.

ISBN 978 0 7524 8049 7

Typesetting and origination by The History Press
Printed in Great Britain

Contents

It's the unseen hand that slips into your own
The non-specific presence that drifts through the home,
A shiver down your neck when there's nobody there;
The slamming of a door and the creak on the stair.

It's the tap on the window, just a branch in the wind?
The drip of a tap into the dry bowl of the sink,
In darkness, in light and beyond comprehension,
To shatter the nerves and grip us with tension.

Acknowledgements

MANY thanks to the following for help and support whilst writing this book: my parents, Ron and Paulene; my sister, Vicki; my wife, Jemma (thanks for the surreal road trip!); my nan, Win; and granddad, Ron; James Mitson; Christopher Cassidy; Susie Higgins and Soul Searchers Kent; John Vigar; Charles Igglesden; Andrew Green; Sean Tudor; The Why Files; The History Press; Francies Moore; Peter Underwood; Joe Chester; *Kent Messenger*; Tunbridge Wells Library; English Heritage; Sean Croucher; Steve Baxter; all the pub landlords and staff who I spoke to; Medway Archives; Bygone Kent; BBC News; the *Telegraph*; *This is Kent*; *Ludington Daily News*; the *Kent and Sussex Courier*; Tunbridge Wells Tourist Information Centre; and all the witnesses who came forward to report their experiences.

'No county in England can boast so many mysterious figures of the night as the Garden of England. Sober citizens of its cities, towns and villages are all speaking of "spirits" they have seen – in dark country lanes, unfrequented passages, in the grounds of old mansions, and in the mansions themselves.'

The Leader Post, 1 July 1935

Introduction

It's the man dressed in black and the woman in white
Or a child dressed up for a Halloween fright.
It's the campfire crackle and the hoot of an owl,
A phantom coach and horses, spectral monk in black cowl.

ROYAL Tunbridge Wells (according to the website 'Visit Tunbridge Wells') was 'the place to see and be seen amongst royalty and the aristocracy'.

For more than 400 years the town has been popular with visitors, who, since the early seventeenth century, have flocked to savour the healing properties of the chalybeate (pronounced 'ka-lee-bee-at') spring which was discovered by Lord Dudley North in 1606. The magical waters can be experienced up to this day, and are served by a 'dipper' dressed in appropriate costume. The iron-rich properties are said to cure all manner of ailments and diseases, as well as hangovers and infertility. The website adds: 'Word of the new spring and its special properties soon spread, and visitors from London and elsewhere flocked to the small settlement which developed alongside the Spring and later became known as Tunbridge Wells.'

The spring has a characteristic red colour, and is slightly warm. One legend states that, many years ago, the Devil, whilst pestering Sussex, was sent packing by St Dunstan: he clamped the Devil's nose with a set of blacksmith tongs and made the horned one flee to Tunbridge Wells – where he proceeded to dip his burning nostrils into the cool waters for relief. A less dramatic version of events claims that St Dunstan, in order to cool his red-hot tongs, walked to Royal Tunbridge Wells and plunged them into the spring.

Imagine the scene, some three or more centuries ago, when aristocracy would visit the wells for a morning sip of spring water and then be on their way to the decorative promenade. During the Georgian period Tunbridge Wells became a popular spa resort. Today it is lined with coffee houses, bars, and the like, and, for a relaxing day, one can still pretend to be a dandy from days of yore and soak up the atmosphere of the place. Like the town of Rochester and the city of Canterbury, Tunbridge Wells is atmospheric in its antiquarian glamour. From the old creaking buildings to grand family houses boasting stunning architecture, the town is rich in history. The year 2009 served as the 100th anniversary of Tunbridge Wells as a 'Royal' town. The town achieved its title in 1909 when King Edward VII, impressed by the town as an attraction to aristocratic visitors, granted the prestigious honour.

Royal Tunbridge Wells sits at the northern edge of the High Weald. Almost 60,000 people reside in the town, though Tunbridge Wells isn't without its green spaces: the town is surrounded by dense woodlands, spacious commons and rolling fields. Dunorlan Park stretches for almost 80 acres and Bedgebury Forest – which slips into Goudhurst, Hawkhurst and Flimwell – is an ancient woodland that takes up some 2,600 acres. It forms part of the High Weald 'Area of Outstanding Natural Beauty'. The former is mentioned in the Anglo-Saxon charter of AD 841. In his *Account of the Weald of Kent*, from 1814, T.D.W. Dearn writes that the town, '[is] a large and populous hamlet lying in the several parishes of Tunbridge, Speldhurst, and Frant, at the distance of 36 miles from London.' He adds that it is divided into four districts: Mount Ephraim, Mount Pleasant, Mount Sion and The Wells.

In 1956 the town suffered a bizarre summer ice storm. The August Bank Holiday Monday tranquillity was disturbed by a barrage of hail which left the streets of Tunbridge resembling Arctic tundra – or, as the local newspaper put it, like 'a rice pudding spreading throughout the town.' So severe was the storm that the rooftops of some buildings collapsed due to the weight of ice. Even more bizarre was the fact that at Tonbridge, just 5 miles away, locals enjoyed the sun and were completely unaware of the freak storm that had hit their neighbours. The severity of the storm echoed a destructive tornado scare which struck Tunbridge Wells in 1763. Pembury and Paddock Wood were caught in the path of the 5-mile wide phenomenon – trees were uprooted from the ground, houses were crushed and animals were battered to death by the enormous hailstones.

I write this as a brief blanket of Kentish snow begins to thaw, and at night the shadows play tricks on the mind as they are cast long across the pristine white by stark, reaching trees. The wintertime is perfect for ghost stories – such tales seem to lack atmosphere when told during a bright summery day! Around the festive season, into the months of a new year, the countryside is crisp, and early morning jaunts bring swirling marsh mists and dew-damp fields; as the curtain of dusk falls, nature comes alive and the senses are heightened.

Royal Tunbridge Wells and the surroundings villages confined within the district are full with ghost stories, perfect for a moonlit night. It's no surprise. Pick up a majority of ghost books pertaining to Kent and you'll read about a handful of local spectres, especially those said to haunt the Pantiles – a beautiful walkway ideal for shopping and relaxing. These ghost stories are relatively well known, almost to the extent that they compete with the village of Pluckley - situated near Ashford - for the title of 'Kent's most haunted location'. Over the last few decades a number of researchers have looked into some eerie Tunbridge Wells yarns, and a few are mentioned here, but my aim is to uncover a new wealth of spooky occurrences – the more obscure, the better! These tales stretch back many years, and many appear here for the first time – though certain ghostly tales, of course, cannot be avoided: they are embedded in the framework of those old buildings. And yet there will be other yarns less well-known, from tales of hideous ghost hounds and other supernatural beasts to haunted castles and creepy roads - all perfect fodder for a cosy night by that crackling campfire. This book is by no means an exhaustive catalogue of Tunbridge Wells' levels of high strangeness, as there are so many weird stories to relate, but it is a selection of my favourite ghostly tales from the town and its surrounding villages.

Whether you believe in ghosts or not, there can be no doubt that many folk love a mystery. So come with me now: pay your fare and hop on this ghost train into the heart of Tunbridge Wells, and prepare to meet a host of tantalising terrors which inhabit this wondrous yet extremely haunted place.

Neil Arnold, 2013

Benenden

The Man-Faced Dog!

I begin this volume with one of the most bizarre entries in this book. It comes from the atmospheric pen of Mr Charles Igglesden, who writes about Benenden in his second volume of *A Saunter Through Kent with Pen and Pencil*. Benenden is a quaint village and civil parish in the Tunbridge Wells district. The village name derives from an Old English word meaning 'Bynna's wooded pasture'. In 1086 the village was recorded as Benindene. The current spelling of the name has been in existence since 1610.

Igglesden describes a disturbing apparition within the vicinity of Skull's Gate Farm – which sounds like the perfect setting for a macabre tale! The farm 'lies just off the Cranbrook High Road'. Legend has it that, in the murky past, a man was murdered in the area under 'revolting circumstances'; his fetid ghost is still said to lurk here. However, this is no ordinary haunting. One day, during the early 1900s, a man was riding his bicycle on the lane toward Skull's Gate Farm when, to his horror, he noticed that he was being followed by an alarming manifestation. According to Igglesden, 'the shape of the ghost was remarkable' – some would say far-fetched. According to the tale, it had a 'long body' resembling a dog but a human head! A sinister tale indeed …

Had the terrified witness observed a hellhound, those frightful, demonic dogs of legend with salivating jaws and fiery eyes? Such fiends are said to take on many forms and colours; some are said to drag chains around their necks, whilst others are bereft of a head. Folklore states that those

Benenden – haunted by a hideous man-faced dog!

11

unfortunate enough to encounter such a ghoulish manifestation are soon to suffer a death in the family.

On 29 December 1672 Benenden suffered a great tempest, described as a 'very great light, to the amazement of all the inhabitants.' Hideous thunderclaps reverberated across the sky, and so severe was the winter storm that those who remained in the village, 'wished themselves farthest from it.' One wonders if the storm was so bad that even the phantasmal man-faced dog had to seek shelter!

The Oldest Road—Ghost Story Ever Told

The county of Kent has so many haunted roads. Tales of phantom hitchhikers, spectral jaywalkers and eerie accident victims abound. One of the best-known road ghosts of the county haunts the village of Blue Bell Hill near Maidstone – for more information, read my *Haunted Maidstone* – but one of my favourite stories – and certainly one the oldest accounts of a road spectre – is briefly mentioned in Charles Igglesden's aforementioned volume. He begins:

Leaving [Benenden] by the way of the Rolvenden road, we pass on the left Pullington, the residence of Captain Neve, and Beacon Hill, so named on account of its having been one of the hills upon which beacon fires were lighted to warn of the approach of the great Spanish Armada.

The name Pullington recalls a strange and somewhat weird story well-known to the older inhabitants …

According to his book, it was once said that a local man named Hunt (who was also known as Fullington Hunt) resided in the area. He was due to marry a young lady named Peggy. The problem was that Mr Hunt was not a trustworthy soul, and he was known to have affairs. Indeed, Mr Hunt had an affair with Peggy's own sister – and married her instead. Young Peggy only found out about the affair on the day of her wedding; upon hearing the bells of the church ring out, she set off merrily – only to find the happy couple at the altar. Peggy forlornly trudged to the nearby pond, which was situated at Eaglesden, and threw herself in. It's no coincidence that the water hole became known as 'Peggy's Field'.

Many years later the unfaithful Mr Hunt, whilst riding home late at night from Cranbrook market, got the shock of his life when his jilted bride-to-be suddenly appeared beside him. Thereafter, the spectre would haunt Mr Hunt every time he travelled on that stretch of road – her spectre would hop on board his cart, and there remain until he reached the stables.

On a lighter, more comical note, it's worth mentioning that Princess Anne went to Benenden School in 1964. It was here, so it is said, that she was mildly spooked one night by a ghost, an apparition which turned out to be her friends playing a prank!

Bidborough

Phantom Monks

The village and civil parish of Bidborough has a population of under 1,000 and sits north of Tunbridge Wells. Parts of the church of St Lawrence date back to the tenth century. During the twelfth century the building was extended. In July 1998, in the vicinity of St Lawrence, two visitors observed a trio of ghostly monks which floated down the pathway at a quick pace. Although the stunned witnesses fled the churchyard, they noticed that the hooded figures had a strange hue about them – particularly under their cowls, where their faces should have been.

St Lawrence church at Bidborough is haunted by phantom monks.

Brenchley and Matfield

A Peculiar Past

The parish of Brenchley – which has a population of fewer than 3,000 people - can be found 8 miles east of Tunbridge Wells. The name is said to derive from an Anglo-Saxon leader whose name was Braenca, and the area his people lived in was a clearing, or 'leagh', in the forest. Over time the village has been called Braencsle, Brencheslega, Branchelegh and Brenchesle. The church in the village – All Saints – dates back to the thirteenth century and the main street which runs through the area is said to be one of the finest in England. The village is famous for its timbered Elizabethan houses. A tree which stands alongside the old Rectory House is said to be 'so ancient that it is mentioned in the Domesday [survey]'. The tree has a girth of 36ft.

Both Brenchley and Matfield have a curious history. One of the first ever diphtheria outbreaks occurred there, and a few centuries ago the country lanes of a night were frequented by highwaymen. On a road to Pembury from Matfield, it is recorded that an isolated spot became known as Beggar's Hollow. Many people were robbed at this location and it was deemed an unsavoury place to frequent if you were not of the criminal fraternity.

The aforementioned church sits close to an avenue of 400-year-old yew trees. Between 1367 and 1370 Edward III was said to have felled more than 150 oak trees to aid the restoration of Rochester Castle. Interestingly, there is a legend in Brenchley pertaining to the cutting down of oak trees:

Brenchley – a place of mystery.

14

in the past it was said that anyone who cut down an oak tree would die within a year. This was proven when, in 1863, the wife of a farmer felled a roadside oak. Although she planted a sapling near the very spot, she was dead within the year. On 19 August 1763 a terrible storm raged over the village. Within thirty minutes the area was completely flooded. Enormous chunks of hail fell from the sky. They were described as being 'like fragments of ice and of irregular shape'. The rector of Barming noted that hailstones measuring 4in were still being picked up ten days later.

A tombstone in the village has a rather macabre inscription on its face. It reads:

'This world is like a city, 'tis full of crooked streets,
Death is the market place where all poor mortals meet.'

Haunted House – For Sale!

On Thursday, 29 July 2004, BBC News reported that a war poet's birthplace was up for sale: Weirleigh, a 'neo-gothic mansion on the outskirts of the village of Matfield', was put on the market for £800,000. The building, which has a ninety-two step staircase, was the birthplace, in 1886, of poet Siegfried Sassoon. The building was constructed in 1866.

The house is said to have a ghost – thought to be that of Sassoon's mother – but the owners at the time, a Mr and Mrs Wheeler, dismissed the legend. Lisbet Wheeler added: 'Mrs Sassoon had eczema. She excluded everybody and people were intrigued.' She would often cover herself in white soothing cream to treat her condition – and so, when she appeared at the window, many visitors and passers-by were spooked. Despite their scepticism, the Wheelers kept the legend alive by hanging a white African mask in one of the windows. Even so, the *Telegraph* of 17 July 2004 commented that the house was known to schoolchildren as the 'haunted house' or the 'Scooby Doo house.'

It seems the ghostly legend may have originated from the pen of a Robert Graves, who stayed at the house in 1916. Shortly after Siegfried's brother, Hamo, died at Gallipoli, Graves heard strange noises such as 'rapping' and 'diabolical yelling' at the house. These bouts of high strangeness were also blamed on Sassoons' mother who, at the time, had been trying to contact her departed son via a seance.

The Churchyard Ghost

Brenchley's All Saints church is said to be haunted by a Roman soldier. During the summer of 1988 a man visited the churchyard. Whilst he was inspecting the tombstones' inscriptions, under the glare of the sun, he felt a presence nearby. When the man looked up he was startled to see the head and shoulders of a Roman soldier. The witness reported that the figure wore a 'close fitting helmet', and 'looked young and fair of face'.

The spectre appeared to be staring at a gravestone. However, when the witness approached, the figure, like so many ghosts, disappeared.

All Saints church at Brenchley.

Ghosts on the Road

The village has a haunted stretch of road. The Maidstone Road was the setting for a road-ghost encounter on 11 December 2009 when a male witness, at 6.35 a.m., was forced to brake hard when two figures suddenly rushed out in front of the vehicle. The figures vanished within seconds.

Haunting at the Halfway House

In September 2011 the *Kent & Sussex Courier* newspaper ran the intriguing headline, 'Pub's spooky secrets are to be unlocked'. According to reporter Elizabeth Barrett, after several weird occurrences at The Halfway House in Brenchley, a ghost-hunting team was sent in to investigate.

According to the newspaper, the pub, situated on the Horsmonden Road, 'has long been rumoured to be haunted by spirits and both locals and former landlords

have witnessed first-hand strange and inexplicable goings-on within its walls.' The pub, which dates back to the seventeenth century, is a former coaching inn, and was once a morgue. The current landlord, Richard Allen, was quoted as saying, 'I've personally not witnessed anything but there have been a number of reports from others. There does seem to me to be too many people who say they have experienced something here to completely pooh-pooh it.'

Poltergeist activity was frequently reported in the pub. One member of staff found that her perfectly laid tables had been upturned, and chairs had been strewn about the place. The *Courier* also reported that a former barman had had an unnerving experience just before closing time one night: 'a tankard began to move mysteriously across the bar of its own accord then smashed on the floor.' One of the pub chefs also had a weird experience one night. While he was turning off the lights in the bathroom, he heard the bar bell suddenly ring – even though the bell had been removed some time ago. The newspaper added, 'Current barman George Bowles, 20, said: "I've heard a lot of stories. I was once in the cellar and thought I saw something but other than that I haven't seen anything at all. I don't really believe it at all, but when I'm here on my own I do wind myself up about it".'

Despite the scepticism of some members of staff at The Halfway House, including Mr Bowles, he was all too keen to speak about a former chef who claimed to have heard coffins – or what sounded like coffins

Halfway House, Brenchley's haunted pub.

– being dragged upstairs one night! A local man named Michael Noakes, a regular of fifty years standing, told the reporter that there had been reports in the past of a spectral old lady at the pub.

Investigative team Ghost Search UK, headed by Donna Gearing, were sent to look into the strange happenings at the pub. She told the *Courier:* 'I went there a few months ago and the minute I walked through the door I felt it was a nice place with no low entities. It seemed quite a busy pub for spirits.' Donna claims to have sensed three male energies in the cellar, and elsewhere in the building she picked up on two children, the spirit of a woman and a further three male spirits.

The report concluded with Donna's thoughts on the nature of ghost-hunting: 'I'd love to catch a full ghost manifestation on film and would love the spirits to step forward to give people evidence. If we can open up people's minds that there is life after death that will be half the battle won.'

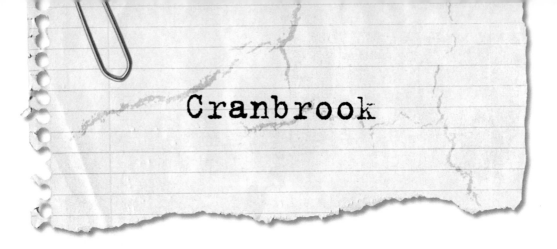

Cranbrook

Spirits Aplenty

In the 1700s a Mr John Russell, who resided in the village, had some sheep stolen by a man named Pullen. On the 1 April, therefore, Pullen was executed. However, Pullen's friends were so incensed that Mr Russell had 'pointed the finger' that they dug up the corpse of their friend from a grave in Maidstone and brought it to Cranbook. Once in the village they shovelled a hole near the window of Mr Russell and buried Pullen.

From that moment on Mr Russell began to go insane: he spent endless nights awake, fully expecting to see the ghost of Pullen rise and seek revenge.

During the same century smuggling was rife throughout the Weald. Thomas Munn, one of the most famous smugglers of the eighteenth century, was born in Cranbrook. Meanwhile, one of the members of the infamous Hawkhurst gang – Bernard Woollett – is said to be buried in the parish churchyard. The gang ran riot for many years until they were captured in 1749. Strangely, the smuggling gangs produced two types of spirit in Cranbrook, for not only are the ghosts of such criminals said to loiter in the darkest corners, but there's one quirky story regarding another set of sprits.

'Many years ago,' wrote Igglesden, 'the gutters in the High Street were filled with spirits in a remarkable way.' Large quantities of contraband spirits were often seized by the local authorities, who would tip it from barrels into the streets. Legend has it that alcohol such as brandy ran like a river into the gutters; locals would take to the streets with pails and bowls hoping to scoop up the drink. So abundant was the illegal alcohol in the streets that many locals would spend the evenings staggering around drunk.

Glassenbury Ghosts

Glassenbury House, the 'seat of the Roberts', is an old lodge. It was originally constructed by Stephen Lodge, although it was rebuilt in 1473 and again in 1730. It sits between Cranbrook and Goudhurst. The name 'Glassenbury' is said to mean 'watery or glassy place.' A member of the Roberts family is said to haunt the avenue where

Left: *Glassenbury Road, the location of a once haunted house.*

Below: *St Dunstan's church at Cranbrook.*

her husband died; he was thrown from his horse as he galloped out to his honeymoon.

Igglesden also mentions how the woods around the house of a night often took on a weird appearance and these moods would have certainly been responsible for 'strange imaginings.' The legend of the area is that of a ghost of a virgin wife 'who was years ago married, amid a scene of revelry, to a gallant of the period.' After the wedding banquet, as was custom, the new bride and groom mounted a horse and rode off on their honeymoon. However, with the couple radiant and jolly upon the horse, they didn't expect the agile animal to slip on the mossy, mist-caressed ground. As the horse tumbled, the groom was thrown violently and killed, but the bride survived with minor injuries. And so the story goes that her forlorn spirit wanders around the grounds, searching for

the ghost of the sweetheart she married and became widow to in one short day.

Chills in the Church

St Dunstan's is the Anglican church of Cranbrook. It is often called 'the Cathedral of the Weald'. Sadly, due to extensive renovations over the years, little remains of the twelfth-century heritage, but the ghost story attached to the building is certainly old.

Above the south porch there was once a room known as 'Baker's Jail' or 'Baker's Hole'. John Baker (1488-1588) was an English politician who also served as the Chancellor of the Exchequer. He was also known as the 'Bloody Baker' due to his brutal prosecution of Protestants. Legend says that the groans of the prisoners who were held here can still be heard. However, Charles Igglesden seems sceptical of such a ghost story, adding, 'I'm afraid it's only rats; but there is nothing like a weird tradition of this sort. It helps you a lot in telling this story.'

Although John Baker died of an illness in his bed, there is another Cranbrook legend which claims that 'the infuriated mob captured Sir John Baker, placed him in the old prison over the porch, where he had incarcerated so many others, collected faggots and finally burnt him alive in the market place.' Some would say that it's the scorched screams of Baker that can be heard in the vicinity on certain moonless nights – but, as is often the case, it depends on who you hear the story from!

Angley Ghosts

The ghost of a witch named Jennings is supposed to haunt the entrance to Angley Park, as is a smuggler ghost, a chap who was said to have been shot at Sandhurst and trudged in agony all the way to Glassenbury, leaving a crimson trail behind him. The man eventually died of his wound and his comrades were said to have dragged him off to the woods to bury him. The ghostly smuggler and his spectral comrades still haunt the spot. Many of these criminals were said to have been hung in chains in the woods as punishment for their sins and then subsequently buried.

Angley Lake is near a smaller water hole and also an overgrown, albeit small,

Angley Park, once home of a supernatural creature.

mill pond. Bizarrely, this hole is said to harbour a dragon. The story is said to be ancient. Of the beast, it says: 'on certain or uncertain nights of the year it wings its flight over the park and pays a visit to the big lake yonder.' According to the tale, the dragon only ate unfaithful lovers. So, should you be strolling through the wooded corridors of the park, especially if you've mistreated your loved one, beware the jabberwocky!

The haunted Pest House on Frythe Walk.

The Pest House Pest!

Situated at Frythe Walk is a house with a haunted history. Built in 1369 as a cottage (although some argue that it may have been constructed several centuries later), it's one of those abodes where one wishes the walls could talk. In the past it has been a hospital used to house plague victims, and a hospital again as recently as the eighteenth century. According to author W.H. Johnson, 'In his book, *The Plague House Papers,* Robert Neumann acknowledges that on the day of his moving in, his cleaner told him that the couch in front of the fireplace was "in the path".'

In the path of what? Well, of a ghost, of course!

The resident ghost was said to travel the route where the sofa was. Like most old properties, the attics also had a sinister atmosphere about them – in fact, the cleaner refused to enter them, and on the day Robert moved in even the removal man was hesitant to go into the loft. Neumann believed that the inner attic room was haunted and many of his visitors to the property remarked on a non-specific presence. One visitor, an American chap, commented that one night, as he was drifting off to sleep, he was disturbed by eerie moans which were clearly not made by his wife. When the man peered into the gloom he became aware of a presence – and then a middle-aged woman carrying an oil lamp glided by the bed his wife was sleeping in.

On another occasion a businesswoman, who had been offered a bed in one of the upstairs rooms, wrote to Neumann after her stay to say that the spirit of an elderly woman had come into her room. She also stated that a voice had mysteriously appeared over her own as she recorded some notes on her tape recorder. The spectral voice had said the words, 'Eight pounds, oh, oh, eight pounds.'

These mysterious words were explained when Mr Neumann delved into the ghostly riddle. He found, according to W.H. Johnson, 'an old document of 1578' which 'revealed that some years earlier the governors of the local grammar school bought the property for use as a school.' Michael Benenden, who had sold the house for £44, had 'insisted on the inclusion of an annuity for the unmarried daughter of the said seller, who shall also have the use of the house, during her natural life.' However, five years later, with her father now deceased, Theresa Benenden's £8 annuity ceased. She put a petition to the Queen but was rejected. Dejected and desperate, Theresa went down into the cellar of the Pest House and hanged herself. Ever since her suicide her portly ghost has frequented the building.

Writer and legendary ghost-hunter Peter Underwood spoke of several people haunted by the 'Pest House Pest': 'In 1970 a Mrs Irene Newton, baby-sitting for the current occupants, twice claimed she saw the figure of "a lovely lady" appear in the inglenook fireplace.' The figure drifted across the room but faded as it reached the stairs. On another occasion, in the mid-1970s, the Deane family reported several bouts of paranormal activity – strange creaks, eerie moans, and then a sighting of a 'tall lady' made by the son, William, in his bedroom. He also saw a ghostly couple who appeared on the landing and prevented him from descending. When the boy walked by them and looked back, they had vanished.

The Caped Ghost

According to the website 'Paranormal Database', on 29 September 2011 a couple driving towards Marden from Cranbrook were startled when a cloaked figure leapt down from a tree into the road and then bounded over their vehicle. As the caped phantom jumped over the car the 'whoosh' of its cloak could be heard. Such an agile phantom brings to mind the legend of Spring-Heeled Jack, a cloaked, fire-breathing spook who haunted London in the 1830s, and was then seen all over the world for the next century. The spirit got its name due to the way it leapt, as if with springs on his heels.

Five Oak Green

The Woman in Black

Although Five Oak Green is close to Tonbridge it is within the Tunbridge Wells district. The King's Head pub, situated on Badsell Road, at Five Oak Green is said to be haunted by the ghost of an elderly woman dressed in black. The woman also wears a large cameo-style brooch.

Occupants of the pub know when the figure is up to its tricks because items such as jewellery and lipstick go missing. The spectre is also blamed for the creaking floorboards and the locking of doors which have been left unlocked by the owners.

'There is no doubt that this place is haunted,' said the landlord to Peter Underwood some years ago. 'I never

The King's Head public house at Five Oak Green.

believed in ghosts until I came here but there's no other explanation.'

A dark shape had been seen drifting across the saloon bar, but the most unnerving experience for the occupants and staff was the shuffling noises heard coming from the locked and empty rooms upstairs. To add to the sinister nature of the sounds, the activity nearly always took place in the dead of night. On one occasion several members of staff conducted a night-time vigil in the area of the back door after a series of strange knocks had been heard. The witnesses jumped out of their skins when a banging noise appeared to emanate from both sides of the door. The cellar – as in most ghostly tales – also seemed to attract the invisible presence, and things in the cellar would often rattle and bang even when there was no one there. Were all the inexplicable bouts of high strangeness connected to the woman in black, or were separate entities to blame? A previous landlady named Mrs Hardstone described seeing a 'dark shape' on one occasion, but one of the weirdest bouts of activity took place when a decorator, who'd left his materials in the building overnight, returned the next day to the room to find that the ghost had done a spot of whitewashing!

Frittenden

Haunting at the Bell & Jorrocks

The village of Frittenden (the name derives from the Anglo-Saxon name *Fridda ing dene* – a woodland pasture of the Fridda family) in the Tunbridge Wells district was first mentioned in a charter of 804 under the name Friddingden.

In the times of Queen Mary, a local miller and his wife, according to the local website, 'both of the Protestant religion, were accused of selling corn cheaper than they were supposed to. They were tried at Sissinghurst by 'Bloody' Sir John Baker as heretics and were burnt at the stake on 18 June 1557 in Maidstone.' A rather harsh punishment, it would seem!

In 1970 the village church of St Mary was struck by a bolt of lightning. Historian John Vigar wrote of a strange legend about this church, commenting that St Mary's is 'the only church I have found where someone's hand was buried in the wall during the nineteenth-century rebuilding!'

The village is also known for its fabled treacle mines – non-existent mines created by the imagination of locals in the 1930s

to tempt rich, sports-car driving London folk to travel all the way to Kent as part of a wild goose chase.

Situated on the Biddenden Road, The Bell & Jorrocks (which began life as the Bleu Bell) pub is an eighteenth-century,

The Bell & Jorrocks pub at Frittenden.

Grade II★ listed building. The first owners of the pub were the Lepper family. In 1983 the pub became the owner of an unusual artefact: a propeller belonging to a German Heinkel plane which was shot down on the outskirts of the village in 1940. The Bell & Jorrocks has been run since 2006 by the Croucher family. In March 2011 I spoke to landlord Sean Croucher about the ghosts of the pub. He stated that two of his children had reported, when they were younger, seeing a man in their bedroom leaning over the bed. The figure appeared to have a hood over its head and no face was discernible. Sean also mentioned that strange footsteps had been heard coming from upstairs when there was nobody up there.

Goudhurst

A Severed Legend

Described by author Alan Fea as 'one of the most attractively situated villages I have ever seen', and by Igglesden as 'probably the prettiest village in Kent', Goudhurst was once rife with smuggling, to the extent that in 1747 all trade in the village came to a standstill. Goudhurst's churchyard was the scene, many years ago, of a great conflict between the Goudhurst Militia and the smugglers. The Goudhurst Militia were a group of male villagers who united in order to drive out the smugglers that had taken over much of the area. Women and children were sent to a neighbouring village as the men stood their ground in the churchyard. When some of the smugglers were injured, the group fled. A stone in the wall of the churchyard is said to signify the exact spot where one of the Hawkhurst smugglers was killed.

A 'fair lady in her ball dress' has been observed in the old ball room of Twisden Manor, and is said to lean with her left elbow perched on the Jacobean mantelpiece. This sounds like a pleasant spirit – until one learns that in her other hand she clutches her severed head! Some locals claim that an unusual stain on one of the floorboards in the house could well be the spot where the unfortunate woman lost her head. No amount of scrubbing can rid the wood of this ghastly reminder. Like many old houses, of a night Twisden is full of creaks, moans and other 'eerie noises'.

Phantoms of Pattyndenne

Pattyndenne Manor, according to author Andrew Green, was 'once the home of the standard bearer to Henry VIII'. The building, formerly used as a hunting lodge, was constructed in 1480 by the Pattyndenne family. Pattyndenne is a Saxon word said to describe a forest clearing which harbours a swelling waterway. The manor can be found on the Bedgebury Road, and it is haunted. A few decades ago a couple named David and Shirley Spearing resided at the property, and it was Shirley who first experienced paranormal activity. She told author Andrew Green that one day, whilst putting up some curtains, she realised that someone was standing beside her.

She could make out the shape of a man in old-fashioned clothes, but the figure quickly vanished.

Shortly afterwards Shirley saw the same apparition. Builders had been restoring the house at the time, and this led Shirley to believe that the upheaval was somehow provoking this spectre to appear. She stated, 'I was able to recognise that he was wearing pre-Elizabethan clothing, with a short cloak.' The figure seemed to be bereft of feet, until Shirley realised that the ghost was probably standing on a lower level of flooring she could no longer see.

After more sightings – a handful involving those working on the building – the name of Thomas was given to the ghost. The spectre seems to be a friendly chap, but doesn't appear related to the strange, spicy smells which linger in what was once the original banqueting hall. Some believe the smell is a phantom perfume, or possibly the scent of incense burning.

The Monster of Goudhurst

On occasion a story gets you looking over your shoulder as you make the long walk home along those wooded pathways. One such story has become a favourite of mine over the years, and I believe it lives up to the hideous title I've bestowed upon it. Author Joan Forman, who wrote the excellent book *The Haunted South*, speaks of a terrible encounter with a supernatural beast whilst staying the night alone in a Victorian schoolroom in Goudhurst where she used to work and reside. She writes:

My sole encounter with it – and one was enough – was at the beginning of the only summer vacation I ever spent in the place. Most of the staff had departed for far-flung and no doubt exotic holidays, and I found myself working and sleeping alone in the oldest part of the building for about three days until I, too, should leave.

On the second night of her stay, at about 3.00 a.m., Joan woke abruptly and noticed something crouching to the left of the bed, on the floor. Joan was paralysed with fear as she faced the entity. 'It was about two feet in length,' she stated, 'the size of a large cat or a small corgi. It resembled neither of these.'

The phantom had a huge pair of 'nocturnal eyes like those of a lemur' and stared intently at Joan. Its gaze never wavered and the beast seemed to somehow mock Joan with its malevolent expression. 'I stared back, playing rabbit to its snake … I could not move to switch on the light, and in any case the creature itself seemed to emit some kind of glow in which I could see the shape of its face and head and the huge eyes, and a dim suggestion of the rest of its body.'

Joan believed that this creature was somehow ethereal. Its presence seemed to last hours, although it may have only been minutes, and she prayed for the light of dawn. Slowly, with the coming of the morning light, the form began to fade. As it did so, the room – which had dropped in temperature – seemed to regain some of its warmth, and as the creature dissipated to nothing Joan found she could move again.

What abomination had Joan encountered in the schoolroom? 'Some two or three years after this incident,' she writes, 'I met the person who succeeded me on the staff of this school, and was told that she had had a similar experience in another bedroom in the same wing, though in her case the animal had appeared on the window curtains.'

What happened to Joan could be described as sleep paralysis. As the body shuts down of a night, many people describe encounters with bedroom invaders of all shapes and sizes. The most common phenomenon is called the 'old hag', a terrifying episode which usually involves a witness who is sleeping on their back. Suddenly, usually between the hours of midnight and 3.00 a.m., they wake and realise that they cannot move – and that there is a presence in the room. This entity, which approaches the bed, is often described as looking like an old crone or witch. The being is said to sit on the chest of its victim, causing a crushing sensation. In other cases witnesses see no entity but describe a great, crushing weight upon their chest. The form only fades when the witness is able to move. Witnesses say that it feels something akin to fighting for their soul.

So are these manifestations simply spawned from nightmares? It seems unlikely when one considers how many people suffer this event each year, but there is no way to know.

The Star & Eagle pub at Goudhurst – once the haunt of smugglers.

The Star & Eagle Spook

This public house and hotel can be found on the High Street in the village, close to St Mary's church. The building dates back to the fourteenth century, and during the eighteenth century the notorious Hawkhurst gang used the pub as their headquarters. The smugglers used to travel to and fro by way of a tunnel. However, in 1747 the Goudhurst militia was formed and rebelled against the robbers, and many of the devious villains were said to have been killed. Legend has it that the echoes of injured men fleeing can still be heard in the now bricked-up tunnel.

Groombridge

The Phantoms of Groombridge Place

The village of Groombridge has been described as a 'picture postcard village'. Groombridge straddles the Kent and Sussex border and is 4½ miles from Tunbridge Wells.

The forest includes the wonderful Groombridge Place, once recorded as a Saxon settlement. Manor houses of varying guises, dating back to 1239, have graced the site. In 1604 the estate was purchased by Sir Thomas Sackville, the Lord Treasurer of England. In 1618, due to a gambling debt, Groombridge Place was sold to Mr John Packer. The present-day house was built by Richard Packer in 1662. In 1994 the gardens to the house were opened. People flock to the area, and children especially enjoy the woodland trails, playgrounds and variety of wildlife.

During late September 2009 a woman named Sarah, who resides at Rochester, visited The Enchanted Forest Nature Reserve in Tunbridge Wells with her partner Darren and their children. The haunting in question took place in the vicinity of the giant chess board. Sarah filmed the family day out at Groombridge Place. When the couple returned home and watched the recording, however, an eerie voice made itself known on the camcorder as she zoomed in to her eight-week-old son. The voice, which seemed to come from nowhere, groaned, 'I'm alive'.

Glorious and ghostly Groombridge.

Groombridge Place – haunted by an ostler.

There was no one else in the vicinity that could have been responsible for such a creepy message.

Sarah told *The Sun* newspaper, 'I've got no idea what it could have been. It was so clear. It sounded like there was something right next to me.'

The video, which can be viewed on YouTube, is one of thousands which claim to show evidence of a ghostly voice. The whispered rasp is down to interpretation – some have argued that it is simply some type of background noise that has been distorted. The 'Kent Online' website briefly covered the tale, with reporter Jo Earle making a brief video of her ghost-busting jaunt at Groombridge Place. Roly Rickcord, director of Groombridge Place, was interviewed about the ghosts of the area. He stated that the owner of the building had put up a £100 reward for anyone who could capture the spook on video. Rickcord added, 'Certainly there is a history of a ghost here'.

The main ghost story related to Groombridge Place concerns a phantom ostler (a person employed at an inn or stable to tend the horses) who, dressed in a rust-coloured smock, is seen standing in the doorway of a building that backs onto the moat. Legend has it that, in 1808, an ostler drowned there.

Sir Arthur Conan Doyle was said to have visited Groombridge Place during the nineteenth century and partook in seances here. Indeed, his novel *The Valley of Fear* is actually set at Groombridge, although it appears under the name 'Birlstone Manor' in the book. In his last published work, *Edge of the Unknown,* Conan Doyle states that a friend of his, a Mrs Wickland, saw the ghost of David Fletcher – the ostler in question – whilst they and their spouses strolled through the area. He wrote:

I took them to the old moated grange of Groombridge, which is mentioned by Evelyn in his diary. As we stood looking at the lichened brick walls, a door which gave upon the deep moat opened and a woman looked out. Then it closed again. We passed on, and I thought no more of the matter. As we walked through the meadow which led to the high road,

The author outside Groombridge Place.

Mrs Wickland kept glancing back. Presently she said:

'There is such a strange old man walking beside us.'

'What is he like?'

'He is old. His face is sunk forward. His back is hunched. He is earth-bound.'

'How is he dressed?'

'He has knee breeches, a striped vest, and quite a short coat.'

'Whence did he come?'

'He came through that door that opened.'

'Then how did he cross the moat?'

'I don't know, and I don't know what he wants, but he is at our heels.'

The group then visited the Crown Inn for a cup of tea but once again Mrs Wickland observed the presence.

'He is there,' she commented, staring at the empty seat beside her.

She added, 'I did not in the least want that second cup of tea, and the extra slice, but he was so close to me, and would have taken possession and helped himself if I had not done so.'

When the group – consisting of Conan Doyle, his wife and the Wickland couple (Mr Wickland being a doctor) – returned home to the Conan Doyle residence, they retired to the garden – where something very peculiar happened. Conan Doyle noted, 'Before our eyes she changed in an instant into a heavy-faced, sullen old man, with bent back and loose, senile lips. She choked and spluttered in an effort to express the thoughts of the control.'

Mrs Wickland, now seemingly possessed, blurted in gravelled voice:

'I am from Groombridge. My name? Well I don't feel clear in my mind. Yes, yes, I remember. It is David. And Fletcher. That is it, David Fletcher. Yes, I have been in service there. Horses. Yes, it was horses I looked to. What year is it? I don't know. My mind ain't clear. Is it 1808 or 1809? What d'ye say, 1927? Well, well, that's a good 'un.'

The Crown Inn was visited by author Sir Arthur Conan Doyle … and a ghost!

With that, the spirit began to look at its body – only to see the form of Mrs Wickland. The spirit, confused by its state of limbo, then claimed to have been pushed into the moat.

'It was Sam,' remarked the spectre. 'But I held on to him, I did. And he came in the water, too.'

'David,' commented Mr Wickland, 'You have got to realise that you are dead. You were drowned that time you fell into the moat.'

'Well I never,' responded the spirit of Fletcher. 'That's a queer idea.'

Dr Wickland attempted to send the spirit on its way to the light. Over the next few minutes Mrs Wickland's body began to straighten.

Conan Doyle concludes, 'Have I not said truly that the actual experiences of the Spiritualist, of which this is one in a hundred, are stranger far than what I should dare to invent? Is it all a fairy-tale? How about the change in the medium? How about the ostler's dress so accurately described? It is not a fairy-tale.'

Groombridge Place is also said to be haunted by a mysterious woman in grey. No one knows who the spirit could be. Phantom smells such as lavender and cigar smoke have been recorded from the main staircase. For the record, the Crown Inn public house at Groombridge dates back to the late sixteenth century. Celebrity chef Jamie Oliver named The Crown one of the top 100 pubs in the South East.

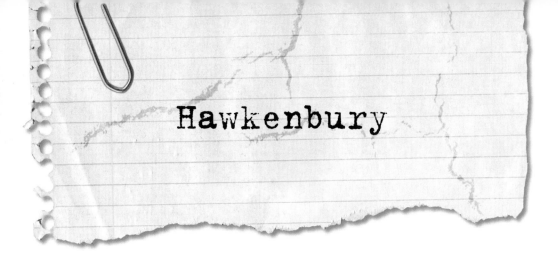

Hawkenbury

The Spread Eagle Spirit

Originally known as Hockenbury, this village, which sits in the district of Tunbridge Wells, but is in the borough of Tonbridge, has a haunted pub. The Spread Eagle – which can be found on Forest Road – is said to date back to the sixteenth century and is one of the oldest buildings in the area.

Highwayman Dick Turpin was said to have visited the inn. The resident ghost is said to be a happy manifestation. The pub's website adds that the wraith 'has been heard, laughing heartily, by many a visitor – so, when you visit us, listen, it's said to be lucky to hear him!'

A Ghostly Investigation

A few years ago a group of psychic investigators known as Soul Searchers Kent visited an undisclosed building at Hawkenbury. Susie Higgins, founder of the group, wrote, 'When we arrived at this very old property, which was once a Hall House, we could feel energies outside and looking at the house we could feel the energy around it.'

When the team entered the building they witnessed a female form looking from the outside in. The group then ascended the staircase and sensed the presence of a man. However, the spirit did not seem eager to loiter.

The team then entered the attic where paranormal activity had been recorded by the owners of the property. Once inside, several members of the team heard an almost disapproving growl and the camera microphone managed to pick this sound up. Susie added:

Suddenly it became apparent that the man haunting this area, and the upper part of the home, was a minister wearing a black cassock, which had a pleat down the front, with a white cloth around his neck crossed to two points at the front. His build was broad-shouldered; his hair was thinning but bushy over his ears. He was an angry man who had sinned many times and was a very corrupt minister. He had no conscience. He hid in the corner because he knew his fate. He hid to prevent having to go to the other side and face his jury, his sentence.

Then, as the team were about to leave the attic, one of the members, Charlotte, let out a petrified scream. She said that a man had rushed by her and growled in her ear. Although the attic was in pitch darkness, a photograph taken by Susie shows the black cloak of a figure entering the attic. The team performed a cleansing ritual of the room and successfully managed to move the angry spirit on to the light. However, there were more ghosts at the house to deal with. Susie explains:

The Spread Eagle pub at Hawkenbury.

Further on into other rooms we sensed that this home had seen five different families over the centuries … The name Johnny was repeatedly shouted at us. I then sensed a female called Alison who we made contact with. She was from around 1866, with a blue dress with petticoat underneath and blue bodice and golden ringlets. A great deal of sadness was felt and incarceration was sensed. She swished her dress around the room, but constantly looked out of the window. She was around 28-30 years old, 5ft 4in.

She talked about watching the swallows in the summer and the horse and carriage coming to the house. A black horse was sensed, but a very nasty man ill treated her and kept her prisoner within this room. She had had a baby that had died in that room. A French man was present with the initial 'D'. This man inflicted pain on her and this was channeled through [Soul Searchers Kent member] Alex, who

felt the pain and suffering. We witnessed a beautiful orb dancing around us and a green mist moving in and out of the room. We performed our clearing for her to release her of entrapment. Moving on to other rooms we heard banging and something metallic moving quite close to us. One room we sat in made us feel very sick, to the point that we had to leave it. [By] talking to the owner we found out that the room was used as a sanatorium for sick children. We cleansed and blessed the room which then felt much nicer and brighter.

The team were called back on another occasion to the Hawkenbury property and picked up the presence of 'small, skinny, hunched, grouchy man' in one of the outbuildings. This individual was reported as being abusive to members of the team and when Soul Searchers Kent left the location his spirit remained.

Hawkhurst

Spirits on Tap

Hawkhurst sits on the border of East Sussex, within Tunbridge Wells. The village is officially an Area of Outstanding Natural Beauty. The name Hawkhurst is said to derive from the Old English *heafoc hyrst*, meaning a wooded hill frequented by hawks. The Domesday Book records the area as Hawkashyrst, but by 1258 the village appears as Hauekehurst. By the early seventeenth century it became known as Hawkherst.

The village is known for its smuggling connections and the reputation of the feared Hawkhurst gang from the eighteenth century. Between 1735 and 1749 it was believed that some 20,000 people were operating as smugglers throughout the land. Legend has it that the local men who could no longer afford to feed their starving families turned to the illicit trade. Ghosts of smugglers are said to roam the lanes of a night, and many of the local buildings, including inns which had connections to the gangs, are also said to be haunted by such figures.

The Oak & Ivy – a local inn – is said to still bear the graffiti carved into the beams by the local gang, who used the building for their headquarters. The smugglers would also use tunnels, which ran beneath the public houses, to conduct their covert operations and transportation of goods. Evidence exists of tunnels running from the Oak and Ivy to the Queen's Inn and Royal Oak. 'A ghostly pair of legs,' says the village website, 'sticking down from the Queen's inglenook fireplace are reputed to belong to a smuggler who suffocated while hiding from the Customs officials.'

According to Peter Underwood a spectre is said to haunt the Royal Oak,

The delightful village of Hawkhurst has a smuggling history.

The Oak and Ivy pub, once a smugglers' haunt.

The Royal Oak pub has a haunted room.

which can be found on the Rye Road. One of the rooms at the building is called 'the haunted room'. Many years ago, a man met his death there. The figure, up until the 1980s, was said to walk through the staff quarters and disappear into a wall. Underwood adds:

In May 1984 I spoke to the landlord but he knew nothing of any ghosts for he had only just moved into the mellow inn. A few days later I visited the Royal Oak and he showed me the haunted room and

said, not knowing anything about any reputed ghost, he had put his son and a friend in Room 22 for the night …

It seems that in the night the two boys got a fright: the next morning they rushed downstairs to report that they'd seen a mysterious set of eyes watching them. The eyes appeared on both sides of the window, and then a dark figure drifted across the room. According to Underwood, staff at the inn had given the ghost the name of 'George'.

The Clawed Creature

During the August of 1983, two brothers, eleven-year-old Mark and nine-year-old Peter, had a terrifying encounter whilst playing in their back garden at Slip Mill Road. At around 7.30 p.m. they observed a peculiar creature fall from a nearby tree. The beast, whatever it was, had been large enough to unnerve the children. Eventually, the police were called, but their search of the area proved fruitless. The only trace of the alleged beast seemed to be large claw marks on the bark of the tree. When one of the witnesses was questioned he allegedly told police that, 'the animal was bigger than our dog (which weighed 60lb) and was covered in shaggy brown fur, and had long black claws.'

Judging by the terrified reaction of the youngsters it seems unlikely they had perpetrated a hoax. At the time the story became known as the case of the 'Hawkhurst bear', but it seems unlikely that such a creature had been prowling the wilds of Kent. Even an escaped wild animal

In 1983 a strange creature terrified two brothers at Slip Mill Road.

of this nature would surely have been sought out after a thorough search. Mind you, two years previous to this, on London's Hackney Marshes, a group of boys playing in the virgin snow claimed they'd been approached by a bear-like creature. Police could only find mysterious footprints in the snow, but around the same time two dead bears were found in the vicinity. Had the Hawkhurst boys seen an escaped animal or some type of beastly phantom? The mystery remains unsolved.

Horsmonden

Healing Horsmonden

The village of Horsmonden – once smuggler country and known for its iron industry – is situated in The Weald, and belongs to the borough of Tunbridge Wells. It harbours a large green called The Heath and each year Gypsy Horse Fairs take place there. The name of Horsmonden is believed to derive from the Anglo Saxon *hors bunda denne* – 'the Horse farmer valley'. According to author Charles Igglesden, Horsmonden is one of the most beautiful villages – despite once suffering at the hands of the cruel plague, and harbours 'several chalybeate springs', said to be iron-rich waters with healing properties.

Igglesden, writing in Volume XVII of his fantastic *A Saunter Through Kent With Pen & Pencil* series, notes, 'a gloomy building known as Scott's Memorial' (also known as Scott's Tower) where he states that one would 'expect to hear the owls hoot around the gloomy spot at night and wood elfs [*sic*] spring from the thicket close by.'

The Smuggling Spectre

With so many smuggling connections in this part of town Igglesden mentions also an area called Gibbet Lane. It is a sombre place where the body of a smuggler was dangled as punishment for his crime and where he now haunts. The spot is the sort of area at night where the rattling of chains has been heard and in the past Igglesden was told by a Colonel T. Kelcey that as a boy he'd been staying in the village and had been 'affrighted by the blood curdling story'.

Gibbet Lane in Horsmonden. A ghostly smuggler haunts this road.

The Unseen Horror
of Horsmonden

The following tale was submitted by a lady named Francies Moore. 'During the late 1990s,' she shares:

> I spent some time staying with friends of my mother, who live at Horsmonden. At that time they had Labrador dogs and one of the dogs they kept was a bitch called Tilly. Unfortunately Tilly did not have the usual Labrador temperament, and was a very fierce dog who thought nothing of snarling at you if she did not like what you were doing. Tilly did not like cats and if she saw one while being walked, all hell would break loose.
>
> One evening – I think it was spring – I was alone in the house for some reason and Tilly was in the garden. Suddenly, I heard her scratching at the back door and barking to be let in. I went and let her in, and she shot past me. I went into the lounge and sat on the settee, and Tilly came in and sat close to me, trembling all over. She stayed like that for nearly an hour, obviously in a state of great fright. As you can imagine, I was not happy to be alone in the dark countryside with a once-fierce dog now reduced to a nervous wreck.

Francies never found out exactly what Tilly had encountered in the garden of the Horsmonden property. However, during the same stay Francies had a peculiar encounter with a strange creature: 'I went into the kitchen one night ... the light was on and the fanlight above the large window was open. I went across to the sink, when suddenly a monster appeared at the window. It was an insect, but a huge one ... It must have been 4-6in long.'

Francies described something akin to a Maybug, though it was far larger than any specimen recorded in the United Kingdom:

> It had two large compound eyes, feathery antennae, and was greenish. It had four wings, the top two being wing cases like a beetle has; they were spread wide to allow the true wings to expand. These true wings were each about four inches long and looked like the wings of a fly only much larger.

After a short while it fell backwards off the windowsill and disappeared. Francies, terrified, fled from the kitchen.

Had Francies simply seen something akin to a moth, or was this some type of unnatural invader? Such a spectre brings to mind several accounts from across Britain of seemingly supernatural insects: one such manifestation made itself known at the famously haunted Borley Rectory, situated in Essex. The 'insect' became known as the 'Borley bug'.

Lamberhurst

The Creep of the Castle and the Abbey Anomaly

Lamberhurst, like so many others in the region, has strong smuggling connections. Its church – St Mary's - is said to have stood for more than 1,000 years. On 7 September 1896 the spire was struck by lightning. Chronicler Edward Hasted wrote that the name Lamberhurst derives from the soft clay of the soil and the large wooded areas of the village: 'Lam' is a Saxon word signifying soft clay, and 'Hurst' means wood. The village has also been known as Lamhurst.

Scotney Castle has the Gothic splendour of many haunted properties. It was constructed by a Roger Ashburnham to withstand attacks by the French. The Darrell family owned the estate for more than 350 years. Scotney has an intriguing ghostly legend. It is claimed that one of the Darrell family – a chap named Arthur – faked his own death during the eighteenth century, possibly after some sinister connections were uncovered relating to the murder of a revenue officer. Arthur Darrell was said to have appeared at his own funeral – no doubt a sight that terrified those in attendance! One mourner claimed that a figure, dressed in black, appeared beside him and stated, 'That is me they think they are burying!' Legend has it that when his coffin was opened, in 1924, by a sexton, it contained only stones. Some claim that Arthur was a smuggler, and that he had killed a revenue officer and thrown his corpse into the moat of the castle. Ever since that moment, people have described seeing the spectre of the officer rise from the murky depths, covered in weed, and taking to the pathway

Scotney Castle sign.

Scotney Castle – haunt of a murderer?

which leads to the front door of the castle. The sodden wraith is then said to bang on the door – no doubt seeking the long-gone spirit of Arthur Darrell. A fantastic spectral tale! I wonder if, in the spirit world, the tormented revenue officer got his revenge on his elusive murderer.

Another theory put forward regarding the wraith is that the figure may well have been one Father Blount. From 1591 to 1598, Blount, a Jesuit missionary, conducted secret services for Catholics; in the sixteenth century Catholicism was illegal. He would often hide in priest holes in the building – such holes were created by Thomas Darrell – but one Christmas Blount was found out. However, despite a search by the local authorities, he could not be found within the confines of the property. Blount – aided by staff members, and the fact a terrible storm raged over head – had escaped the castle and swum across the inky moat, and was never seen again. Maybe the ghostly figure – dripping wet – is that of Father Blount, returning to the building to dry off and carry out his services?

In October 2011 someone visiting Scotney Castle photographed a strange mist in the grounds, but it's more likely to be their breath floating across the air and camera lens on an autumnal day, rather than a wandering spirit. Another legend states that a former owner of the castle, named Betty, wished for her ashes to be sprinkled in the grounds of her castle. The person who took the photograph suggests the form could well be the ghost of the woman. We'll never know …

The castle is also said to have another ghost, one responsible for eerie whispering and ghostly footsteps. Peter Underwood believes that this spectre could well be that of Walter de Scoteni who, in 1259, was persuaded by William de Valence to administer poison to the Earl of Gloucester and friends as they dined at a banquet in the Bishop of Winchester's abode. Many died from the poison, but the Earl escaped death (though he did lose his hair, teeth and fingernails). Walter de Scoteni was hanged. Some say it is his ghost that loiters in the building. After all, his family name gave the castle its title.

More recently, a woman named Jenny reported that she had been overwhelmed by a feeling of depression whilst standing near the lake (moat). 'We [Jenny and her husband] made our way back to the car and went home. I did ask if they had any ghosts. There was nothing they knew of, but I believe somebody in the past had been murdered or drowned in the lake.'

Nearby Bayham Abbey, once home to the Premonstratensian Order, is said to be haunted by spectral monks – some say twelve, although the number seems to vary. These phantoms wear white habits, which would tie in with the strict order above – the white canons, a reformed sect of the Augustinians. Also, unlike many ghostly monks, these are not silent. Instead, their presence is made known by the ringing of their bells and their eerie chants. The procession has been seen to travel around the cloisters and the old ruins of the church, moving in pairs as eerie mists that fade into the haze of dusk. Although these are benign spirits, to see such a sight of a night must be an alarming spectacle.

A few decades ago the Ghost Club paid a visit to the old ruins. One of the members reported the presence of 'a holy person, a monk or an abbot,' but the experience lasted only a few seconds.

Thankfully, the ruins are closed off to the public after teatime and so the processions are left to their devices. Another ghostly noise said to emanate from the ruins is the sound of an unseen choir. On certain nights it is said that the singing spooks can be heard from far away, the tones drifting on the evening breeze. The smell of incense has also been experienced by some. I visited the abbey ruins in April 2012 and spoke to two members of staff who stated they'd not heard of any unusual encounters regarding phantom monks and ghostly noises. However, one member of staff did mention that a few years ago a man, walking near the two children's graves in the ruins, had frozen with fear. He was unable to move for a short while. After he broke from the seemingly supernatural spell he had to sit down to recover.

A few yards from the ruins you will find Bayham Abbey Dower House, which may be haunted by a ghostly couple. A member of staff told me that a few years ago two separate witnesses reported seeing a ghostly man and woman glide through one of the rooms and disappear into the fireplace.

The Headless Horseman

Charles Igglesden writes of a creepy Lamberhurst phantom from an area once known as Ballard's Lane. The story, which seems to originate from the 1800s, states that a headless rider, mounted upon a white horse, is said to gallop up and down the stretch of road on certain nights. No one knows why the rider is bereft of his head, but according to Igglesden, 'It is a significant fact that no one can be found who has actually seen this unfortunate apparition.'

The Ghost Car

Judging by old records, Lamberhurst is an extremely haunted place. One such ghost is said to be a phantom vehicle that has also been seen around Bells Yew Green and Hook Green. One morning in 1997 a female witness named Lynn Smith had an encounter with the ghost car on Bewl Bridge. She was travelling on a treacherous stretch of road when suddenly the headlights of a vehicle came speeding towards her. Lynn pulled over by the side of the road with haste but the car never came, despite the flash of lights and the roar of its engine. Poor Lynn seemed to be the target of several supernatural experiences before and after this experience. She used to live in a building called Court Lodge and reported several bumps in the night. The old manor house would have banging doors, creaking floorboards and curtains which seemed to fall down even though they were secured. Lynn's report of the ghost car of Lamberhurst certainly wasn't the first.

On 12 March 1915 the *Kent Messenger* reported on the 'Phantom Vehicle':

After accounts circulated last week of a phantom vehicle being seen by Colonel Leland of The Clearing, Hawkhurst, and his chauffeur, the Colonel has kindly supplied us with an account of his experience: 'I had to go back to the Depot to do some work after dinner, about 9 p.m. My own car, allotted to me by the WD, and my driver, Webber, a soldier, were waiting for me, and I left the house a few minutes after nine. We had gone two or three hundred yards when I noticed a moving light on my left; concluding that it was a horse-driven vehicle coming into our road, I told Webber to slow down and let it come ahead. This was done and the vehicle, which was very indistinct, drew in and turned the way we were going. I told Webber to go up behind it and not pass. He did so and we kept close behind it for about two hundred yards. I could plainly see the back of the vehicle, which was black and appeared to be a hearse; it was moving at a trot. The queer part was I could see no driver and the two panels at the back and the keyhole for locking the doors showed up most distinctly under the rays of our lamps. When he got around a corner, I said to Webber, 'Push on.'

We did so and the road before us was empty. We accelerated but there was nothing to be seen and Webber said, 'Lord, sir, what was that?' We went down and around Sunbury but did not see any vehicle. I can assure you that the vehicle, whatever it was, only rounded the corner a few yards ahead of us and there was nowhere it could have gone.

In his book *The Ghost Hunter's Road Book,* John Harries speaks of 'an old-fashioned black limousine' on the main stretch to Sussex. He claims that the vehicle is only seen 'by the driver of a vehicle moving on the same side as the parked limousine', and that it is invisible to any oncoming motorist. Another report claims that in 1978 the custodian of Bayham Abbey had been told by several visitors that they too had seen the phantom car.

Furnace Mill – in 1908 strange goings-on were reported here.

Who Moved the Horses?

One particularly odd story that has existed in Lamberhurst folklore was reported on in the *Daily Mail* newspaper on 28 May 1908, under the heading, 'Unusual Haunting in Kent':

> The stables of Mr J.C. Playfair at Furnace Mill, Lamberhurst, Kent, have been disturbed several times this month by an unseen force. One morning, the horses were found to have been turned the reverse way round in their stalls, their tails in the mangers and their heads in the stalls. One horse was missing and later found in the hay room nearby. A partition had been knocked down to get it out and the door of the hay room was barely wide enough for a man to enter. Other phenomena included the removal of some heavy barrels of lime which were hurled down the wooden stairs; a large water butt too heavy for any human being to move overthrown; and locked and bolted doors found open. Two watchdogs were on guard at all times and had not reacted to the mysterious disturbance in any manner.

Members of The Ghost Club visited the mill on one of their investigations. An article by an Adrian Harland, submitted to *Bygone Kent*, commented, 'During the early years of this century Furnace Mill became a notorious place for ghost-hunting. The then owner, Mr Tom Playfoot, had reported certain unaccountable happenings and manifestations in the old mill house and about the farm'.

It seems, however, that when the *Daily Mail* sent a reporter to the now infamous farm, Mr Playfoot was reluctant to discuss the alleged haunting. It seems that people from far and wide were arriving, much to the disgust of Mr Playfoot. However, it was good business for the village: postcards showing the 'Haunted Mill' were being sold at a regular rate. Mr Harland believed that the mischievous spectre responsible for the strange happenings was none other than Mr Playfoot's young son, Tom. It seems that the boy had become so immersed in a book about ghost stories that he decided to play a prank on his father. He could not, of course, realise that the hoax might backfire and cause people to invade the property.

Chills at The Chequers

Andrew Green mentions this haunted pub in his work *Haunted Kent Today*. The building dates back to the twelfth century, when it existed as a manor house, but it has been an inn since 1414. The ghost here is said to be a woman dressed in red.

She has been seen quite often, even up until recently. Strangely, however, only female members of staff have been privileged to observe her. One morning a young female member of staff walked into the dining room and saw the figure peering from the window. It turned to look at her and then vanished before her eyes. As Andrew Green put it, 'Local historian Ian Peters heard evidence from a previous landlady that once she heard footsteps going up the stairs, but was assured by her husband that there had been no one to account for the sound.'

The ghost has also been blamed for the moving around of furniture.

A different ghost appears to haunt what is known as Room Four. As in the case of many haunted rooms, sudden

The Chequers pub at Lamberhurst is haunted by a woman in red.

drops in temperature are recorded here and strange noises such as tapping have been experienced. Guests have refused to stay in the room, stating that the freezing atmosphere and peculiar noises disturbed them greatly. One witness who was brave enough to spend one night in the room claimed that an invisible presence had attempted to climb into bed with him. No wonder that the next day he demanded another room!

Another ghostly tale concerns a former barmaid who reported that one night, just before midnight, as she was perching in front of the till in the main bar, a woman with long, dark hair, wearing a black top, peered around the dividing door. The bar had been shut at the time – and although there were a few customers chatting, the woman was not one of them.

Poltergeist at the Pub

On 9 June 2009, *This Is Kent* reported on supernatural activity at a pub situated in Lamberhurst. The headline, 'Lamberhurst pub persecuted by poltergeist', referred to The Swan at the Vineyard public house on Furnace Lane. According to the newspaper report, 'A pair of fearful publicans are appealing for information which could explain some ghostly goings-on at their pub'. The incidents involved slamming doors, eerie rustling noises and items which had been thrown across the hostelry and smashed.

A strange blob of light had been captured on the pub CCTV camera one night, leaving pub owner Mrs Saunders to believe that the pub was being haunted by a strange figure. She told the newspaper, 'We had finished work and were sitting at the bar chilling out and chatting when all of a sudden we all turned round for some strange reason. Then there were some strange rustling sounds. We turned the lights off and went up to bed and the next morning there was all this glass smashed.'

Mrs Saunders' partner, Martin Potter, had been sceptical of ghosts previously but even he could not explain some of the events. He commented, 'I suppose there have been a couple of incidents ... [After the first incident] we came down[stairs], and lo and behold there were smashed glasses once again. It makes you wonder.'

Another sceptical member of staff, barman Sean Holland, stated that he was so spooked by the eerie happenings that he refused to lock up the bar on his own. His fears were confirmed by another member of staff, Tracey Young, who believed that the ghost may have been that of a previous tenant who was not happy with the recent alterations to the building. Some researchers into ghostly phenomena believe that any type of upheaval in a building could upset the resident spirit, which may have lain dormant for many years. Tracey told the paper, 'The original landlord here in the 1800s was George and he had a daughter called Mabel. When George passed away his daughter took over as the landlady. They say that the doors opening in the restaurant are George taking care of stuff where the cellar used to be. Things have definitely got worse since Tracey (Saunders) came here. Perhaps she reminds George of his daughter?'

A poltergeist haunted The Swan at the Vineyard pub.

High Street High Strangeness

One house situated on the High Street used to exist as a pub but is now a private house. When it acted as a pub there were several ghostly tales attached to it, including the sighting of a ghostly woman and child by a member of staff in the kitchen area.

The sound of a child laughing has been heard in the old fireplace, and the patter of tiny but invisible feet has also been reported in the past. A former landlord named Adrian Kirkman reported that some visitors who'd stayed at the pub had been awoken in the night by an invisible presence that had tipped their beds up. Author Andrew Green wrote that a historian, John Moon, had traced the presence of a ghostly woman to the early part of the eighteenth century.

A Lost Soul at Lindridge Place

During the mid-1980s a Mr and Mrs Dutch resided at Lindridge Place – a Grade II★ listed building that dates back to the sixteenth century. One day, whilst the owners were away, their gardener, a Mr Bryant, was pottering around the place and decided to make himself a cup of tea. Suddenly, the family dog began to bark and headed off toward the main hall. Mr Bryant followed the agitated animal and, according to Andrew Green, 'was shocked to see a woman leaning against the chimney breast of the inglenook fireplace.' The figure slowly faded from view. When Mr and Mrs Dutch came back from their holiday, Mr Bryant was hesitant to tell them about the spirit until the New Year. However, when he did finally mention his sighting the couple didn't seem too bothered about the ghost: in fact, they rather enjoyed the possibility of having an invisible resident! No further experiences took place until two years later, when Mr Dutch heard footsteps at the top of the stairs and then a terrible crashing noise. However, a search proved fruitless. Some believe that the ghostly woman is a lady named Miss Japp who lived at the house before the Second World War. Miss Japp had been found dead in the area of the lavatory, which was located at the top of the stairs. Interestingly, a crockery cupboard was near by, suggesting that Miss Japp may have dropped, or fallen, into the crockery when she died.

Langton Green

Woman and Child

Langton Green can be found just 2 miles away from Tunbridge Wells. Springs of pure water were found throughout the village although on dark nights some of the lanes were best avoided in case one should be accosted by a highwayman. One area which harbours a spring is Gipps Cross, also known as Gibbets Cross, where in the past accused highwaymen and other criminals were hung up in chains so to warn others not to offend.

On a less sinister note, the classic game Subbuteo was said to have been invented in Langton Green. Bizarrely, it is the AA website which briefly mentions a spectre said to haunt The Hare at Langton Green. The pub, situated on the Langton Road, is said to date back to 1785, but the original building on the site, which had been there for almost fifty years, was destroyed by fire in 1900. According to the legend, a ghostly woman holding a similarly spectral child has been seen on the staircase and in the cellar area of this pub.

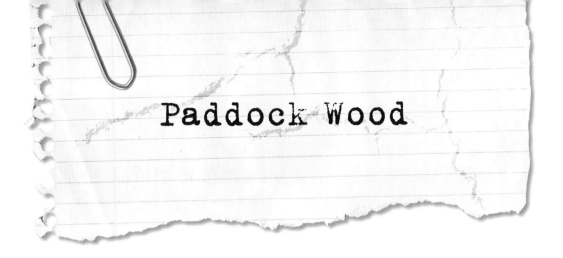

Paddock Wood

Haunted High Street

On 28 October 2011 *This Is Kent*, to coincide with Halloween fever, reported 'Spooky goings-on in the area', with reference to Paddock Wood High Street's Red Cross charity shop.

'The temperature drops massively, books go flying off shelves, toys turn themselves on, we hear footsteps upstairs – we get activity all day long,' commented shop manager Cheri Ellerker.

The ghost is reported to be that of a woman, and this was verified when a psychic medium visited the shop and told staff she could see a woman holding a locket.

'This shop was built on the site of the old Parochial Hall which was dedicated to Mary Horrocks by her husband,' stated Cheri. Could the mystery woman be the spirit of Mary?

Thirty-seven-year-old spiritualist medium Jason Croucher visited the shop in the hope of trying to contact any spirit present. The newspaper reported that the man, who 'investigates paranormal activity for a hobby', picked up a girl, possibly called Abigail, and sensed that she might be looking for something on the premises. Mr Croucher failed to pick up any sign of Mary Horrocks but did claim to sense a male spirit in the upstairs stock room – an area of the shop known for its uncannily cold temperature.

The newspaper covered the story of the shop's haunting after they spoke to local historian Charlie Willard. Although an avid collector of spooky tales, Mr Willard confessed to never having seen a spectre.

Further along the High Street is the Wine Mill off-licence, another reputedly haunted site which Mr Willard had researched. However, shop manager James Byrne commented that in the five years he'd worked there nothing strange had happened to him. He told *This Is Kent*, 'There were rumours of an old woman hanging herself under the stairs, and a child drowning in a well out the back, but I don't know if any of this is true.'

In May 1912 the ghost of an old woman, sometimes known as the 'ghostly granny', was seen on a stretch of road through Paddock Wood. Judging by the reports, the phantom seemed to always cross the road in front of cyclists and then completely vanish, leaving the witnesses spellbound.

The Pantiles

Portico of Peculiarities

The Pantiles – a Georgian colonnade, originally known as The Walks, and then later the (Royal) Parade – was, during the seventeenth century, often frequented by regal characters. Although today it exists as a shopping parade, the modern structure has two things in common with the past: the curative waters of the chalybeate spring, and the ghosts.

The well – whose name derives from the Latin word for steel – is said to hold health-giving waters, made distinctive by their iron properties. The spring was discovered in 1606 by Lord Dudley North, whose physician stated that the waters contained 'vitriol'. North, who lived until the age of eighty, declared that it had been the spring which had given him such a full life. Although at the time the spring was nestled in the undergrowth, the area was soon cleared by Lord Abergavenny and the area was protected. From then on the legend began that the waters could cure, 'the colic, the melancholy, and the vapours; it made the lean fat, the fat lean; it killed flat worms in the belly, loosened the clammy humours of the body, and dried the over-moist brain.'

A verse was made pertaining to the waters, stating:

These waters youth in age renew,
Strength to the weak and sickly add.
Give the pale cheek a rosy hue,
And cheerful spirits to the sad.

The spot of the spring (grid reference TQ5838), situated at the north-eastern end of the parade, is where the Pantiles starts; here also sits The Bath House, built in around 1804. The parade runs from Nevill Street to Linden Park Road. The Upper

The Pantiles – one of Kent's most haunted locations.

and Lower Walks were constructed in the late 1630s. During the civil wars the wells became neglected, but their popularity resumed when, in 1664, Queen Catherine of Braganza, who'd fallen ill, was advised to drink from the spring.

The name is said to derive from the tiles which pave the floor of the Upper Walks. In 1698 Princess (later Queen) Anne donated £100 to have the walkway paved. This happened after her son had apparently slipped on the muddy ground. According to Mary Campbell, in her booklet *A Walk in Old Tunbridge Wells,* Princess Anne returned a year later and, 'finding no paving, she became angry and never set foot there again.'

Little has changed since the eighteenth century, although during the late 1700s – when the area was called The Parade – the Pantiles were removed and replaced with stone flagging. It took until 1887 for the name to be revived.

On 28 October 2010, *Your Tunbridge Wells* reported 'Spooky goings-on close to home in west Kent'. It mentioned a couple of Tunbridge Wells ghost tales for the fireside. The source stated:

Site of the 'healing spring' at The Pantiles.

As Halloween fever grips the nation this weekend, it's worth remembering there are lots of things going bump in the night rather closer to home. According to local folklore, the Pantiles, in Tunbridge Wells, are home to more than twenty ghosts. Such is the Georgian parade's ghoulish gaggle, regular walks are staged to give people the chance to learn of the spooky goings-on. And it's not just recently the tales have taken hold. It was

way back in 1835 mentions of ghosts at the Swan Hotel first surfaced and there are even supernatural tales related to the beginnings of the town's famous spring, dating back as far as 1606.

… Graham Bell, of Upper Grosvenor Road, who wrote the local booklet *Pantiles Ghosts,* even claims to have spotted a ghost himself. 'About a month ago I was in bed at 3 a.m. and was rudely awakened,' he explained. 'I saw a lady with icy grey hair leaning over my bedside table. She had a nightdress and a cardigan on. She disappeared very suddenly and I just lay there thinking "yes, at last!" Whether

View along The Pantiles shopping parade from the Nevill Street end.

it was a figment of my imagination I don't know. Like most ghost stories you are never too sure you didn't dream it. However, there are various things that convince me it's not just my imagination.'

The article concluded:

Mr Bell explained this was not the first time he had experienced a ghostly going-on and said the week before he had also spotted a face looking over him and remembered waving his hand through it. 'You never know if it is just a shadow or something but this is the third incident in the same room,' he recalls. 'My bed is in the same position as the very first inhabitant of my home and I think she died. I am the third occupant and the person before me seemed to want to get out really quickly. I am elated to have finally seen one.'

Whilst speaking of Upper Grosvenor Road it's worth quickly deviating from the Pantiles' path and noting another intriguing story. A woman named Deirdre Morris reported that when her husband David passed away, numerous odd things began to happen in her home. A chessboard, which belonged to her husband, seemed to be the main focus of the drama. The pieces on the chessboard would move about in the night. On another occasion Deirdre found her sink full of rose petals – David's favourite flower was the rose. Journalist Jack Pleasant visited Deirdre at her home after she reported that she'd found a flower placed next to her breakfast plate. She would often pull the curtains across rather casually when she left the house, meaning a gap would be left, but David would often get cross at this; she believed that, even in the afterlife, every time she left a gap in the curtains her departed husband still returned to make sure they were closed shut to prevent prying eyes.

One of the weirdest experiences Deirdre had had was not related to her departed husband, however. One day, while meditating in her garden, a mental image of a Japanese monk came to her. Suddenly, she leapt to her feet, rushed indoors, grabbed a piece of paper and began writing a series of poems as if they'd come from nowhere.

Deirdre, who has always had an interest in Japanese culture, contacted an expert on Japanese literature. He identified the mysterious verses as something akin to the work of a monk named Ryoken – a monk who had died in 1831! Had Deirdre received messages from the other side? And so, back to the Pantiles …

Ghost-hunter Peter Underwood was intrigued by the legends of the Pantiles, recording, 'The High Street has several allegedly haunted properties including a shop where phantom footsteps walk up stairs that no longer exist; a house where an unidentified lady in a poke bonnet has been seen by successive occupants over a period of seventy years; and a corner property where a ghostly form has been seen looking out of an upstairs window.'

Woods Restaurant & Bar – once the haunt of a spectral horseman.

Josephine Butcher, in her booklet *I Was Born on the Pantiles*, mentions a weird encounter which took place when she was a child. Josephine had been born in a house situated across the road from the Bandstand. 'One time I had been asleep,' she wrote, '... and I woke up and I had a sort of nightmare and I was crying out because I saw in the bedroom a man mounted on horseback.' Maybe it was just a dream, but Josephine was sure this phantom was actually in her small room. She called out to her mother who raced to the bedroom asking what was wrong. When Josephine told her mother of the apparition, it was only natural that her mother should reply that it was just a dream – though Josephine was adamant that the spectre had been more than vivid nightmare. Many years later however, Josephine was told by her mother that, 'There was a rumour that someone saw a ghost there, and it was a man on horseback.'

A strange and surreal time-slip took place almost two centuries ago in The Swan Hotel, which sat at No. 58 – its London Road entrance can still be seen. A Mrs Nancy Fuller had taken her young daughter, Naomi, on a visit to the Pantiles in 1835 and decided to stay; their room was No. 16 in the hotel. As they ascended the staircase Naomi began to act very oddly: she closed her eyes and began muttering to herself. Naomi had never visited the place before, and yet she told her mother that it all seemed familiar. Even stranger was the fact that Naomi then mentioned that her lover was waiting for her in the room. This type of remark, from the lips of a child, seemed extraordinary. Then, when they both entered the room, Naomi

The Pantiles Hotel – formerly The Swan.

walked straight over to the corner and said, 'John'. Her mother could see no one but she claimed that for a short while Naomi seemed to change: her face seemed older and her clothes became old-fashioned. When Nancy spoke to her daughter, she was told by the child that before the building had become The Swan she had lived there. According to Naomi, the building was once known as the High House. When she lived there she had had an affair with a man named John, but her father had disapproved and John was ousted from the town. Naomi also mentioned that she had been locked in the room. Eventually, she was so desperate to see her lover that she decided to conjure an image of him holding her hand. She then leapt to her death out of the window.

It's no wonder that room 16 is reputedly haunted. The tapping sound often heard at the window may be scant evidence of a present spirit but some unseen presence sporadically moves the furniture around and likes to throw the bed sheets about the room. The hotel is also said to be haunted by a woman in grey – one such sighting took place on 2 October 1997.

The Pantiles has many haunted shops. Author Andrew Green, writing in 1999, mentions Binns Coffee Shop, Chalet Arosa Restaurant, and The Gem Shop as all being ghost-infested. Binns Coffee Shop (now occupied by La Casa Vecchia – a Mediterranean restaurant) at Nos 70-72 was said to have been haunted by a woman in a long grey dress (strangely, the adjacent building to the restaurant is now called The Grey Lady). She often appears on the first floor and gazes out of the window. According to Green, some people 'believe that she may be Sarah Porter, an assistant to the fashion king whose duties were to watch out for newcomers to the Pantiles.' However, as is the case with most ghostly tales, other theories have been put forward to explain who this could be. One suggestion is that the ghostly woman is a forlorn bride-to-be who was jilted by her sweetheart, whilst others claim the woman used to reside at the property and has no wish to leave. In the 1990s Binns Tearoom was run by John Bath, who reported:

The old lady – she's been seen by several people. I've been in this restaurant as an owner for over ten years, and in that period there's been at least five people working here that's seen her, including my wife. Prior to that there's been a lot of people that have worked here in the past, going back fifty years, that have also seen her. It's always the same story [and] they always describe her in the same way, in the same dress in the same position. So it really does substantiate that an awful lot of people have seen her.

Mr Bath's wife was apparently jostled by the phantom woman on the staircase. In every eye-witness statement she is described as a woman, around seventy years old, in a crinoline cloak. People never see her face. Mr Bath mentioned how the area where the woman is seen had once been rearranged by unseen hands in the night: a table and two chairs, always put in a

La Casa Vecchia – formerly Binns Tearoom – haunted by a grey lady.

certain position, were found the next day with the chair facing the window, as if someone had been sitting there gazing out. A sculptor named Anthony reported:

> In the winter of 1996 we were gathered here … some fifteen people … one evening, and there was a gentleman who was a medium who was speaking to the audience. I was sitting at the back of the crowd above the restaurant and I saw a figure of a woman appear in the centre of the room. She was wearing a grey, dusky blue sort of veil that covered her head and shoulders. I could only see the torso of the woman and she moved very slowly from the left to the right and disappeared through the wall. I was quite surprised seeing this torso of a woman. It was quite a pleasant feeling: it wasn't at all frightening in any way. She was a gentle person …

John Bath's theory behind the ghostly presence is that during the 1700s the building may have been a house of ill-repute and that the lady was the madam of the house. One girl in particular went missing, and may have had connections with a local man who 'liked the ladies'. The legend of the ghost story is that the old woman still looks out of the window, hoping for the young girl to return to the house.

Mr Bath concluded, 'I think that whenever you get a lot of people and a lot of history you're bound to have got a lot of circumstances which would create ghosts. I think that's why the Pantiles has got so many.'

A property once known as Chalet Arosa Restaurant (at Nos 44-46 but now occupied The Ragged Trousers pub) also experienced paranormal activity. A Pat Humphreys, who used to run the premises, reported that he was asleep one night in the building when he was awoken by a sudden drop in temperature. Shortly afterwards a peculiar, eerie light appeared on the wall and then seemed to take the form of a carpenter wearing an apron. The spectre then glided across the room and disappeared through another wall. The property was said to be haunted up until 1999 when the owners, the Chowdhurrys,

The Ragged Trousers pub – formerly Chalet Arosa restaurant.

reported that objects moved of their own accord and footsteps had also been heard. Pat Chowdhurry, who ran the place as Tiles Restaurant, commented that the building, many years ago, was a gaming room, and that the carpenter ghost had also been seen on the corner of the stairs. Andrew Green also heard that a building known as The Gem Shop (which used to sit at No. 48) was haunted. Green writes, 'Geoffrey Butler, owner of this specialist shop in the Pantiles, told me of an unusual incident experienced by a carpenter carrying out the restoration of the cellar some twenty years ago.'

Number 48 which used to be the Gem Shop.

The carpenter had been having a conversation with an electrician in the building, and the electrician told the carpenter that he would have to go and turn the electrical supply off. In the darkness the carpenter continued chatting to the electrician for some time – but when the lights came back on there was nobody there! The carpenter was sure that he had been chatting with someone who was by his side in the blackness but, when he questioned the electrician later, he found that the electrician had been on another floor of the building. In December 1997 local *Meridian News* filmed at No. 48. The feature, presented by Keith Chegwin, looked into the ghostly sightings of the building. Accompanied by a ghost-hunter, the film crew descended the steps into the dank cellar – though two pets dogs, owned by the occupier of the building, refused to follow. The ghost-hunter stated that an alleyway called Friends Passage was attached to the ghostly presence, and the crew walked into the gloom – and again, one of the dogs bolted with fright.

Number 40 used to be the post office. There is a plaque at the spot to mark this. Numbers 40-44 used to be occupied by the Assembly Rooms, where distinguished folk would attend dances. Richard 'Beau' Nash, a celebrated dandy and self-appointed Master of Ceremonies, would take chair over and supervise the extravagant balls and gaming which took place in the building. Gambling wasn't banned from the area until 1748. The ghostly activity has been reported over the last few decades, with occupiers of the post office reporting phantom smells such as the wafting of tobacco. Interestingly, in Georgian times it was believed that certain rooms of the building were set aside for smokers. Maybe the smoke that lingers is a hint that some of the masters' servants are still waiting – smoking away - for their master to return? Many must have fled the rooms after building up a huge debt due to their gambling ways.

Each year festivities are held on the Pantiles and local people flock to the area to dress up and re-enact the scenes of days

A sign marks the spot of the old post office.

gone by. During the 1990s one shop, at No. 11, stood empty (and at the time of writing still is) and was used to store some of the costumes that people used to wear. A local resident named Robin Addey mentioned a tale: 'The lower part of the shop was used, principally, as a ladies changing room. One of the costumes was a riding habit and staff noticed that the skirt had been lying on the floor but the very next day an antique gun used in the festivities was found lying across it.'

It was also reported that a woman named Stephanie had been alone in the cellar underneath the shop one evening in 1997 when she heard her name being called.

As for a few other Pantiles spooks, No. 7 (The Vintry) is reputedly haunted. The building was erected in 1668 and has been a shop since 1768. In 1996 Julia Millbank and Spencer Ayres reported on a strange, unseen presence in the bedroom of the flat above The Vintry, as well as the moving of objects. On one occasion a friend named James Simpson stayed with the couple and also sensed a presence in the room. More recent reports seem scarce, but there has been a lot of poltergeist activity at No. 9, a nearby building, so maybe the spectre has moved on! Number 9 used to

be the 'Old Butcher's Shop'. The building dates back to 1750, but a butcher's shop could be found at the site up until the 1980s. At 6.30 a.m. one morning in the May of 1996, road-sweeper Kenneth Morgan was passing by properties 9-15 when he was startled by a crashing noise suggesting someone was in the building (which at the time was under restoration). Kenneth could clearly hear the sound of timbers being thrown about and yet there were no builders present. When the workmen finally turned up there was no sign whatsoever of any disturbance. A lady named Jo Morgan, who resided at a flat which backed onto the building, also reported the sounds of objects being thrown about. Her pet dog refused to enter a certain room, and Jo would often be awoken by the bed covers being snatched from her.

A couple more flats which sit above the shops on the Pantiles are said to be haunted. At one location there is rumour of a haunted room where no dog will dare to tread. At another, during the August

No. 11 The Pantiles.

The Vintry at No. 7.

of 1997, a woman reported a spooky encounter whilst in bed. She woke with a start at 2.30 a.m. and walked towards the window. Suddenly she saw, in the reflection of the window pane, the back of a figure. The woman at first thought it was a reflection but this did not make sense as the mystery apparition moved of its own accord. The witness described the figure, who vanished, as having dark hair and wearing modern clothing.

The Coach and Horses pub (now Pantiles Antiques) used to sit on the Lower Walk of the Pantiles, at No. 31. The building dates back to the eighteenth century and was once a very unsavoury place to frequent. Tramps, drunks, smugglers, and thieves would often be seen around the place. In the nineteenth century a local man who had built up a lot of debt managed to save enough to pay back what he owed. However, on the night he visited the pub to meet his creditor he was robbed outside in the passageway – which is known as the Coach and Horses Passage. He tried

to pursue the thieves but to no avail – and so, distraught, he crept back to the passage and hanged himself from a beam by the entrance. Another version claims that the man went upstairs to one of the back rooms of the pub and hanged himself. Either way, legend has it that on certain still nights you can hear the creak of the timbers to suggest that the unhappy soul is still swinging from the rope that took his life.

Judging by its chequered past, it would seem that the building has always attracted ghosts. During the late nineteenth century a family who resided in the building often reported supernatural encounters, such as ghostly smells and fleeting figures. At least three deaths have been recorded at the location, and it would seem that the negative energy still lingers.

Halfway along the Pantiles sits the Corn Exchange. This building, constructed in 1801 as a theatre to gratify the wishes of actress and flamboyant character Sarah Baker, now exists as a shopping parade. Perched above the property is the statue of Ceres - the goddess of the harvest. Many years ago, due to the

Coach & Horses Passage. In the nineteenth century a mugging took place here and spawned a ghost story.

The Corn Exchange, situated on the Lower Walk.

building houses Thomas Tubb Interiors. It is at this spot that horses, en route to London just over 30 miles away, would stop to rest. This spot also seems to be the favoured place of a female ghost dressed in Georgian attire. No one seems to know who the young girl is – but maybe she sits on the stone waiting for a lift from Tunbridge Wells to London? One summer's day a few years ago, Daniela Bayfield – an audio producer – was sitting at her desk when her friend, a man named Stephan, looked out of the window and said, 'Daniela, what is that?' as he thought someone was sitting on the milestone.

boundary of line of Kent and Sussex running through the building, the stage of the theatre was situated in Sussex, and the auditorium in Kent! The ghostly sightings seem quite recent. During the early 1990s there was a report of a woman in Victorian attire gliding through the Tunbridge Wells Exhibition. Other people claim that the mysterious and sudden chills which drift through the building are the result of a spiritual presence. In the March of 2012 I visited the Pantiles and visited the shopping parade. Although it was rather cold, I was more inclined to blame the chill on the cool spring air and the fact the doors were open rather than any possible unseen ghost!

There is a ghost story attached to an old milestone that sits in the town just behind the Pantiles. The weathered stone, which is on an old coaching route on the London Road/Major York's Road junction, can be found near a building called the Master Transcriptions Studio, which used to be the site of Bennett's Wagon Office. The white

I looked out of the window and didn't see anything at first and then there was this figure which appeared. She was about 19. It was really strange because I do not believe in ghosts or anything, but I think there are a lot of things that do occur that we can't explain. All I can say is that it unnerved me. I saw someone looking straight at me as if I shouldn't be here.

A ghost of a young woman has been seen standing by the milestone in the foreground.

Another ghost story from the area concerns the Wellington Rocks, which is one of three sets of unusual sandstone formations in the town - the other two sets being High Rocks and Toad Rock. Wellington Rocks can be found on one of the commons, a few hundred yards from the Pantiles. The land is owned by the Manor of Rusthall and managed by Tunbridge Wells Commons Conservators. The legend is that in 1917 two teenagers named Daniel and Elaine, who worked at the Pantiles, were very much in love, but because of the long hard days they worked they found it difficult finding time to be alone together. When they did manage to sneak away on a short lunch break they would meet at the same time at Wellington Rocks. Daniel knew that his call-up papers for war were imminent and so he promised Elaine that when he was granted some leave he would return and marry her. One day Daniel's mother told Elaine that she had received a letter to say that Daniel was coming home, and Elaine knew exactly the time and place to meet him. On a dark, rainy and windswept evening Elaine made her way to the rocks, but Daniel never came. An hour or so later Daniel's mother came to Elaine, who by this time was very cold and wet, and broke the news: Daniel had been killed in action. Elaine refused to leave the rocks, and when Daniel's mother left she climbed to the highest rock – from which she leapt. She died of a broken neck, and possibly a broken heart. The ghostly legend of the area is that, on certain nights when the wind howls and the rain batters down, the spectre of Elaine can be heard pining for Daniel.

Wellington Rocks – said to be haunted by a young lady waiting for her lover who died at war.

Wellington Rocks attract many visitors and during a warm day children like to climb the huge grey stones to act out their own adventure. I wonder how many people have seen the resident ghosts, or know of the legend? Another story concerning the commons took place in 1965. A Tunbridge Wells man had a frightful encounter whilst with his sister, her then husband and their friend. Kenneth Morgan (previously mentioned), a road-sweeper who spent most of his time cleaning the streets around the Pantiles, never forgot that peculiar night when the group took a short cut across the common from the direction of the High Rocks cricket ground. As they came on to the wooded path they observed a strange mist and then saw two black riders pass by. 'We saw them for about five seconds,' reported Mr Morgan. 'I reckon they were smugglers … the blue hazy mist seemed to follow them.'

Another witness, named Wendy, also came forward to report a phantom horseman encounter. One day Wendy, who worked at the Swan Hotel, was driving along Major York's Road when she pulled over to wipe her windscreen. Suddenly she noticed, on the other side of the road, a horse and rider. The horseman wore a purple cloak and the figure galloped off into the woods.

A few years later a newspaper reporter named Kim Waller was with a friend on the common. As they were sheltering from the storm they saw a large individual approach them. The figure was so large that at first they took it to be more than one person – until it got closer. The figure seemed to be wearing a long grey gown which had frills circling the bottom. When the wraith came within just a few metres of the terrified witnesses it seemed to sink into a squatting position and emitted strange squelching noises. The girls, who by this point had become somewhat bolder, approached the figure, but it faded from view as it moved away. According to Peter Underwood, 'The curator of the local museum was intrigued by the story and suggested that the figure may have been the ghost of a local character, enormous Mary Jennings, a drunkard who died when she was about thirty in 1736.'

The common has had a long and possibly dark history. In 1663 it is recorded that King Charles II's court camped at the common, and an old racecourse used to worm through the land.

York Cottage, on Major York's Road, was constructed on the common in 1830 by the lady of the manor. The ghost said

Several ghosts have been seen on Tunbridge Wells Common.

York Cottage, on Major York's Road. It is said to be haunted by a woman in black.

to haunt the building is a woman in black, and according to witnesses – including people who have lived at the cottage – she is often reported as being seen by the front gate. Despite her gloomy attire, the spirit is believed to be pleasant and often quite happy in her nature. The nearby Swan Garage is also said to be haunted, or at least the flat above it is. One day a member of the Swan Hotel staff was asked to clean out the flat, as it hadn't been occupied for some time. The man draped his coat over the back of a chair and began to work, but when he turned round the coat was on the dusty floor. Thinking it had simply fallen, he put it back on the chair, making sure this time it could not fall off. However, a few minutes later the same thing happened. Shortly afterwards

the man felt that he was not alone in the flat and, looking up, saw a misty female form, dressed in a light-coloured gown, who seemed to float across the room. The spook then completely disappeared.

Another area not far from the Pantiles is Linden Park Road. One house here was owned many years ago by a Mr Dent who reported that, on several occasions, he would hear someone – who he at first assumed to be his father returning home – enter the building, hang his hat on the hatstand, and then enter the lounge. However, when Mr Dent investigated the house he always found it empty. His father would usually return a short time later.

One theory as to why the Pantiles and surrounding areas are so haunted could be the fact that many buildings actually sit on a hidden stream. Ghosts, many researchers claim, are often associated with water, and the Lower Walk has a stream winding beneath it. The fact that so many of the local waters are said to have curative properties suggests to some that there is something very unique about the place. The stream, many years ago, used to act as a border. Some of the buildings were in Kent, but others, just metres away, were considered part of Sussex. Legend has it that many years ago a tramp died in bed in one of the buildings on the Pantiles, leaving his body across the borderline. No one was sure where he should be buried – his legs were over the Kent line, and his head in Sussex!

I think it's fair to say that the Pantiles and its surrounding areas are riddled with ghosts. There's also mention of a big white phantom car – said to resemble a Bentley – that drifts through the town. Couple this with the occasional phantom dog and spectral cat and our gaggle of ghosts seems complete. A few of these phantoms, much the same as those said to haunt the village of Pluckley, have embedded themselves into the local psyche as classic ghost tales, but goodness knows just how many more spirits are attempting to push through the cavalcade to make themselves known to the sensitive eye.

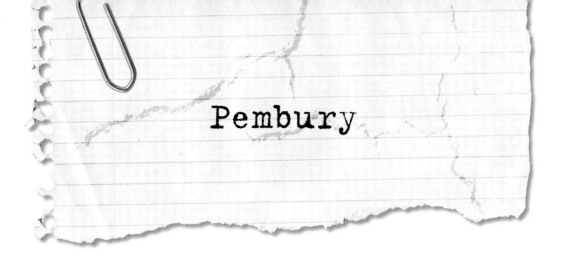

Pembury

Haunted Hawkwell Manor

The name of Pembury may have derived from the Saxon *Pepingbeorg* or *Pepingeberia*, the former meaning 'the hill of the Pepings', the latter meaning the 'Pippin Apple Tree'. The village sits just 2 miles north-east of Tunbridge Wells.

According to the 'Village Net' website, many years ago the owner of Hawkwell died, leaving two daughters and a widow. One of the daughters eventually married and moved to London, where she had a child. However, when the child was three months old the woman, after suffering abuse at the hands of her husband, attempted to escape back to Hawkwell. As she had no money for transport she carried the child all the way home. When she arrived, however, she was horrified to find that the manor had been burned to the ground. Thankfully, the woman, who by this time was weak and weary, discovered that her sister and mother had moved to a nearby abode, but sadly the strain of travel and grief had been too much; she collapsed by the roadside before she could reach them. At the time a party to celebrate her mother's birthday was to

take place, but the old woman postponed it until both her daughters were by her side. Of course, many of the locals in attendance knew nothing of the daughter's trudge from London and told the old woman that her daughter was miles away, and would not be coming. At that point, the mother gasped, 'She *has* come!' She then collapsed and died. Later that night, farmhands walking through the area found the frozen body of the young woman by the charred ruins of the manor house. No one knows what became of the child.

It is said to be her ghost who haunts the area, still searching for her mother and sister.

Bayhall Manor

Bayhall Manor's earliest residents were the Culpeper family and the Duke of Buckingham. In her *History of Pembury,* Mary E. Standen spoke briefly of the haunting – which the newspapers exaggerated in the 1960s – which struck when the structure was a ruin. The ghost is said to be of an Anne West, the last person to live at the mansion. Sadly, ghost-hunters

Haunted Bayhall Manor used to sit at the end of Chalket Lane before it was demolished.

and the like swarmed the unsafe building after the newspaper coverage and the owner eventually had it demolished.

Bayhall Manor was one of those places that 'look haunted'. The location is now occupied by a farmhouse which sits at the end of Chalket Lane – a private no-through road. In his 1907 book *Haunted Houses*, Charles G. Harper wrote of the house, saying 'Great Bayhall Manor-house, long years ago became a farm, and now deserted, has in recent years been the scene of manifestations in the ghostly kind.' One record from the early 1900s in reference to the high strangeness reads:

> The old manor, with its moss-grown roof, its broken doors and windows and its old moat, can be traced back to the reign of King John. For several weeks past persons residing in the immediate neighbourhood have been startled by unearthly noises and groans, and many of the villagers have been heard to declare that they have seen ghostly figures walking about.

'Such has been the sensation caused in Tunbridge Wells,' it continues, 'that a number of well-known gentlemen have visited the house and heard what they believe to be "true spirit noises".'

One of these investigators claimed that whilst conducting a vigil – armed with a stick, just in case he encountered an apparition – he heard a dragging sound, as if a person was pulling a heavy body across the floor. Although two investigators refused to venture forth, some were brave enough to explore the depths of the old building, descending the steps of the cellar – where they heard a succession of groans and thuds. The men fled.

Harper adds: 'The unquiet spirit supposed to haunt this spot and to bring a trail of mystery with it is locally said to be that of a lady whose tomb in Pembury old churchyard is the common talk of the neighbourhood.'

The tombstone reads:

> To The Memory of
> MRS ANN WEST, late of Bayhall,
> In this Parish, who Died April 13th, 1803.
> Aged 34 years.

The above etching seems to be an error, as it is stated by some that Ann West died in the 1830s – and some even say 1903!

Ann, it is claimed, was terrified that she might accidentally be buried alive. Therefore, she requested that her coffin be bereft of lid, and that a hole be made in the framework of the vault, so, should she wake, she could call for assistance. Another legend, as reported by Harper, states that 'she willed her fortune to a man-servant on condition that he placed bread and water on her coffin for twelve months after her presumed decease.'

Great Bayhall Farm House now stands on the spot once occupied by a haunted house.

Ghost-hunter Frederick Sanders investigated the haunting several decades ago in 1939, and one dark night – accompanied by a Kenneth Jeffrey - visited the vault. Sadly, no ghostly apparition stirred, but his torch beam did illuminate a ghastly sight. He noted, 'By illuminating the interior of the open vault, by directing a beam of light from a torch downwards through the small iron grille, I observed the crumbled remains of the coffin and remains of Mrs Ann West. Her skull lay upon the floor of the tomb, minus its lower jawbone.'

Suddenly, Sanders claimed he felt three taps on his shoulder – or was this simply an involuntary muscle movement, coupled with his overactive imagination? Had a droplet of rainwater dripped from a disturbed leaf? According to Sanders' notes, there were no trees nearby, and the 'three taps' were of 'quasi-sensory origin'.

Sanders also recorded:

As we stood near the old tomb a noise like a subdued rustling became audible, followed by a light thump, followed again by jerking, gritty sounds. Turning, we glimpsed a small black form bounding along the pathway. It was a black cat at full gallop and it quickly disappeared into the gloom on the further side of the graveyard.

But had this creature been a phantom or simply a flesh and blood domestic cat hunting mice? The latter seems more likely, a fleeting form made all the more atmospheric by the pen of Sanders.

Horror Hospital

Ghost-hunter Andrew Green wrote that Pembury Hospital, situated on the Tonbridge Road, was home to more than twenty-five spirits. In his book *Haunted Kent Today,* he mentions a relatively recent ghostly occurrence from 1996 involving a Brian Wells, transport manager. The transport office now sits where the hospital chapel was once situated, and it was here that Mr Wells, working late one night, heard a noise as if a horse was neighing. Mr Wells investigated, but to no avail; he continued his work, but then he heard 'the noise of a horse scraping on what sounded like cobblestones'.

According to Green, the next day Brian learnt that the spot where his office was now had, many years ago, been the area where a horse would bring in patients. It is said that the horse, and its cart, were involved in a tragic accident one day: the animal reared up and the cart was shattered, killing the driver.

Pembury Old Chruch – haunted by a ghostly woman.

Rusthall

Weirdness at Rusthall

Rusthall is a village situated 2 miles west of Tunbridge Wells. It is rumoured that the name Rusthall derives from the rusty nature of the local water! The area has several wells said to have healing properties. The area is also known for what has become known as Toad Rock, a weird rock formation said to resemble – yep, you guessed it – a toad.

A website dedicated to the history of Rusthall mentions a couple of local ghost stories submitted by readers of the site. One chap named Franklin has an amazing story to share: 'In about 1976, I saw two ghosts on separate occasions (a soldier and a maid with a candle) [in] Lower Green Road'. The witness was of the belief that the spot once housed a V.A.D. Hospital during the First World War. Another tale, submitted by Francis, mentions a sighting from 1981: 'Whilst walking with a friend from Southborough, through Hurst Woods, he had been startled when the silence of night was broken by the shrieking sound of a horse approaching. The two, fully expecting to be charged by a horse, began to run in terror, but the creature never materialised.'

Another ghostly tale is mentioned by Andrew Green in the vicinity of Mulberry Lake, which is situated on Bishop's Down in Rusthall Park. Green records an account from a fisherman named Tony Tidley, who, with a colleague named Kevin, had a seemingly supernatural encounter one evening as they set their rods up over the pond in pursuit of tench. As the night drew in, both men heard the sound of someone running towards them – but a flash of the torch revealed only the flitter of bats. This happened a handful of times, but no form ever materialised. The old manor house which used to sit on the spot was set fire to during the civil war and the servants, trapped inside, were burnt to a crisp. Maybe it is their tortured souls which are heard flitting through the trees, still in search of a way out of the burning house that no one but them can see?

Pub Phantoms

The Beacon Hotel and Restaurant in Tea Garden Lane has a ghost or two. The building dates back to the late nineteenth century

The Beacon Hotel at Rusthall.

– quite recent, some would say, for a haunted property, though over the years it has seen many residents.

During the Spanish Civil War (1936-1939) it housed six Basque refugees, and then, in 1939, it acted as a safe haven for some Austrian Jewish women who had escaped the clutches of Hitler. The building became a hotel in 1959 but the ghostly activity began a few decades after, with reports of bottles and glasses being hurled across the bar. Footsteps were also heard on the stairs, and during the late 1990s there was a vague report of a shadowy male figure on the stairs. In the March 2011, I spoke to a member of staff named Neil who reported that on three occasions he'd seen the figure of a woman, wearing an off-white cloak, drifting from a small door and disappearing into the fireplace (which is original, and dates back to 1895). His first sighting of the figure took place around six years ago but his most recent sighting took place in 2011. He also confirmed the

sighting of the shadowy figure on the stairs leading to the function room by stating, 'I saw this figure about seven years ago, when I first started working at the pub. The figure appeared to be guarding the stairs and was wearing a police, or prison officer's type outfit.'

In his excellent book *Haunted Inns of Kent*, Roger Long speaks of The Red Lion at Rusthall as being haunted. The pub can be found on Lower Green Road. Centuries ago, horses would trot along this stretch of road and their thirsty riders would often pull up for a drink at the pub. When Roger visited the pub a few years ago he spoke to a co-tenant named Andrew who told him about the cold spots in the pub, and the unseen spirit that seems to like locking and unlocking doors. On one occasion Andrew even saw the back end of a spectral dog – suggesting that some long-deceased pet still likes to frequent some of the warmer corners of the pub.

The Red Lion pub.

Sandhurst

Phantoms of the Ponds

The village of Sandhurst is situated on the Kent/Sussex border. Its name means 'sandy wood'. The 'Village Net' website records that the church of St Nicholas 'was completed by the time of the Black Death in 1348/49'. According to legend, those who survived the plague moved away from their residences near the church; the dead were so abundant in the graveyard that they sought a healthier environment in which to live.

There is a ghost story attached to the two ponds in this village (Chapel Pond and Brick House Pond), recorded by Andrew Green. More than half a century ago a woman drowned herself in Chapel Pond, whilst during the late 1800s a man killed himself at Brock House Pond. On Christmas Eve, 1973, at 8.00 p.m., two men – Brian Lee and Henry Hodd – were strolling in the vicinity of Brick House Pond when Mr Lee was startled to see a gentleman standing in the hedge. Terrified, Brian cowered behind his friend.

Sadly, Mr Hodd, probably due to Brian's sudden panic, never caught a glimpse of the wraith but was told by his frightened companion that the ghostly man was around thirty-five years of age and was smiling. When the two men continued their journey – with Brian using much haste in his stride – Brian claimed the figure followed for a short distance and then vanished. Though this alleged ghost has no direct connection to the suicide victims, it is stories such as these which keep local legends alive.

Another watery legend is mentioned on the 'Friends of Tunbridge Wells and Rusthall Commons' website, with regards to the 'Lost Gardens of Rusthall', a serene area situated at the southern edge of Rusthall. The source adds that if one should visit the three peaceful lakes – which were developed in 1708 by a local entrepreneur – then one may hear about the ghostly Victorian bathers. In life, these figures would have taken a dip in the cold baths which were once part of the pleasure gardens (which sadly no longer exist).

Sissinghurst

Spirit-Infested Sissinghurst

The small village of Sissinghurst, once referred to as Milkhouse Street, sits in the District of Tunbridge Wells, with Cranbrook to the south, and Goudhurst to the west.

On the Sissinghurst Road, Charles Igglesden once recalled an atmospheric ghost story suited to a rain-soaked, thunder-ridden night. 'A weird story', he writes:

> ... is told about the Sissinghurst Road and the entrance to Swifts (a park which used to be a cricket ground) ... Before the old pay-gates were abolished, two coal-black steeds, with fiery eyes and flaming nostrils, attached to a noiseless vehicle, and driven by a phantom coachman, have been seen in the dead of night galloping at a terrific speed along the turnpike road ...

As the spectral animals and their phantom coach hurtle onwards, the gates of the park seemingly open of their own accord and swallow the ghosts. The gates creak to a close to signify the end of the ghostly scene.

Castle Capers

The previous story isn't the only Sissinghurst scare story – far from it, in fact.

Igglesden adds that, as you 'come to a turning on the Biddenden Road', there is said to be the ghost of a phantom coach driven by a ghostly lady, 'one of the victims of "Bloody Baker's" outrages in years gone by.' This spectre is said to appear on a small bridge that straddles a brook. Igglesden states:

> This dip in the hill, with its ghostly legend, is a fitting entrance to the domains of Sissinghurst Castle ... If the wraiths of the wicked frequent the earth as a penalty for their sins, then the spirit of poor Sir John Baker must still be hovering about in hopeless despondency down here by his old castle, and it is not surprising that even now his weary ghost is heard all night prowling about the old ruins, and even playing bowls in the cabbage garden for want of a smoother green.

Sissinghurst Castle – owned by the National Trust – sits nowadays as the remains of an

Sissinghurst Castle – a glorious place with a ghastly history. The beautiful gatehouse entrance to Sissinghurst Castle. Legend has it that 'unfortunate lunatics' were once chained up here.

Sissinghurst Castle

Elizabethan mansion. The gardens (which today are maintained by eight gardeners) were created in the 1930s by novelist Vita Sackville-West and her husband, Harold Nicholson. The land – which originally existed as a woodland clearing – was purchased in 843 by the Archbishop of Canterbury, but by the late twelfth century it was owned by Stephen de Saxenhurste. A manor house with a three-armed moat was built here in the Middle Ages. By 1305, Sissinghurst was impressive enough for King Edward I to spend the night.

In 1490 Thomas Baker purchased Sissinghurst. In the early sixteenth century Sir John Baker – mentioned in the Cranbrook segment – gave the house a new brick gatehouse. Since then, the building has been used as a workhouse and also a prisoner-of-war camp. Charles Igglesden adds, 'And yet, although in ruins, everything – the moat and even the bit of pasture that extends in front of the gateway – and even the old pump on the strip of waste land, have their own special stories.' It is said that under this soil are resting the bones of the French who died as prisoners of war. Igglesden adds that 'coffins have been found in the wood just beyond.'

Today, Sissinghurst Castle is open to the public – as it has been since 1937, when visitors used to pop a shilling into a tobacco tin for entry. Although prices have, obviously, risen, visitors will find the place a tranquil area to explore. There are two lakes, a gift shop and restaurant, an atmospheric library and what is known as The Tower, which was built in the 1560s. One has to climb the seventy-eight steps to appreciate the view.

Another legend states that the wall by the gateway was once used to chain up 'unfortunate lunatics'. Igglesden comments, 'Yes, there are some funny old legends about this place – the most impossible that were ever invented by man.' Another unlikely tale has it that the tranquillity of the area was once broken by 'unearthly shrieks' which 'were many a time heard in the old gateway at nightfall, and, to add to the terror of the inhabitants, many persons were robbed in the adjoining woods, while others vanished, never to appear again.'

A gruesome legend relating to an ancestor of Sir John, Mr Richard Baker – who allegedly murdered many young women near here – exists. It claims that Baker's lover, and her friend, discovered the dead bodies of several women in his home. The young woman's friend then heard a noise outside, and when they both peered out of the window they saw Baker and his servant struggling with the body of another dead woman. The two women were horrified but, despite being stricken with fear, they hid themselves in a dark area under the old staircase. Soon, Baker and his servant came into the building, dragging the corpse with them. The hand of the unfortunate murdered lady snagged in the baluster of the stairs – and so Baker hacked it off, the gory limb falling into the lap of one of the horrified women. Thankfully for the women, however, the murderers did not

see them. When Baker and his accomplice were out of sight the two women fled the building – taking the severed hand with them! When they reached home they told their ghastly story, and the families in the surrounding areas that had lost relatives and friends were notified that such missing persons could well be hidden in the house of Baker. With that, a group assembled, and a trap was set: they asked Mr Baker if he would like to attend a large party. The plan was to have several local police constables hidden amongst the guests. Baker suspected nothing, and attended the party – and it was here that the grisly hand was presented to him. At that point the police officers apprehended him. Legend has it that he was burnt at the stake.

The severed hand may be the reason a dog belonging to Lady Nicholson once froze in fear as it ascended the old staircase with its owner. According to G.M. Dixon in his booklet *Folktales & Legends of Kent*, '[Lady Nicholson] became aware that the animal had stopped. She turned and saw that her trusty friend, who would have protected her from anything, was standing transfixed.' The poor dog was so petrified that the hair on its body had begun to stand on end. Had it seen a spectre, or some ghastly image of the past that had embedded itself into the framework of the building?

Charles Igglesden mentions a reputedly haunted barn not far from the castle, although the sole story attached to it is far from a ghostly tale. One night a local man named Jack Smith, to hide from a raging storm, decided to hole himself up in the old barn but found himself on edge as soon

The Tower.

as he nestled into a dark corner. Suddenly Mr Smith was startled by a drawn-out sigh – and to his horror, in the gloom, he saw the fleeting figure of a person which he took to be a spectre. Jack struck out at the figure with a stick, only to find that the form he had hit had simply been a horse! Some argue that Mr Smith had had one too many drinks that rainy night and that once in the barn his mind had begun to play too many tricks.

Another accident which took place, and one which reminds us of Mr Smith's error, also took place at Sissinghurst and involved a Madame Nairn who occupied Sissinghurst Place (Madam Nairn's mother, Lady Louisa de Spaen, renamed Milkhouse Street 'Sissinghurst'). Madam Nairn always slept with a shotgun by her bedside and

one night, thinking there were burglars slinking through the grounds, she grabbed her weapon, opened the bedroom window and fired at one of the fleeting shadows she had seen on the driveway. No one knows if burglars, or in fact ghosts, were present that night, but the next day the gardeners' wheelbarrow was found on the driveway sporting a rather large bullet hole!

It seems that a number of people in Sissinghurst, many years ago, were afraid of ghosts and other midnight marauders, and sadly their paranoia resulted in not only terrible accidents but also death. The Gate House, which stands 'a short distance out of the village on the Cranbrook road', has a sad legend attached to it. In this building an old man once resided whose livestock had been stolen. A kindly neighbour came by

The grounds of Sissinghurst Castle are said to be haunted by a priest.

one night with a gift of two ducks, but upon hearing the footsteps coming up the drive the panic-stricken chap reached for his gun and fired into the inky night. The next day the next-door neighbour was found lying dead in the garden, staring at the sky.

Going back to Sissinghurst Castle and its ornamental gardens, we hear of the ghost of a priest said to be seen wandering around the grounds. Peter Underwood reports: 'In the 1950s Felix Seward, Chairman of the Ghost Club from 1954 to 1960, knew both Sir Harold and Lady Nicholson and, knowing of his great interest in psychic matters, they talked freely to him about the ghost priest.' Legend has it that, when alive, the unfortunate priest had been bricked up in one of the walls of the building, and

that his footsteps have often been heard pattering about the place. Underwood adds that on one occasion, while speaking with Sir Harold over lunch, he was told that the priest had been seen, heard and felt on numerous occasions – even by Sir Harold himself. These tales were backed up by Sir Harold's trusted housekeeper, one Mrs Hayter, who reported that many visitors had asked her who the 'reverend gentleman' was seen lurking about the place. Mr Underwood also states in his *Ghosts of Kent* that Sir Harold may now also haunt the property. He writes, 'Interestingly enough, Sir Harold had the occasional habit of clicking his teeth with his tongue' – and oddly, since his death a peculiar clicking noise had been heard in some of the rooms of the house.

The House Where Evil Dwells

It's fair to say that, in most cases of allegedly 'haunted houses', residents rarely have to deal with activity beyond the usual bumps in the night – creaking floorboards, cold spots, the occasional fleeting shadow and maybe a family's pet dog or cat behaving strangely in certain corners of the property.

However, when Ian Davison moved into a cottage in the area during the early 1930s, he could have had no idea what he was letting himself in for. When Mr Davison first purchased the cottage, the tricks above began to occur. Davison – who was an actor – attempted to enjoy rural life in Sissinghurst nonetheless, but things grew more and more sinister. At first it was ghostly footsteps, heard on the first night Mr Davison stayed at the house. These strange steps remained, and seemed to patter about the place almost every night. The dog – a Great Dane – would also react with terror to the sounds – and more so when strange raps began to sound on the windows of the house. Maybe someone was playing a prank? Then Mr Davison's friend, a chap named Euan, remarked on the icy coldness of one particular room; the presence of the roaring fire did not affect the chilled atmosphere one bit. Soon, neither man found he could stay in the cold room for long spells. If they did, they would become dizzy. On one occasion Euan had fallen asleep in the room but, when he awoke, he told Ian that he'd had a terrifying dream concerning a person that had crept up behind him and tried to strangle him.

The following night Ian was in the room when it suddenly became unbearably humid.

Despite opening the window, he could not chill the stuffy atmosphere. Both men then felt drowsy, and then Ian collapsed. A strong, pungent odour filtered through the hallway from the room, and again came the feeling of powerful strangling hands around the throat.

Some sceptics would argue that the terrifying nightmares of a strangling presence were simply that – nightmares. However, the phantom footsteps, strange smells, and fluctuating atmospheres continued, night after night. One evening Ian's slumber was disturbed by footfalls coming from outside. When he jumped out of his bed to investigate, however, they suddenly ceased. On another occasion the dog began to growl as the footsteps made their way towards the house. The front door then creaked, the dog whined, and a crashing sound and more steps suggested that two men were running outside. So what makes this different from any other ghost-infested house? Well, for one it is an extremely well-recorded haunting – Davison made daily records of the possible paranormal activity during his three-year stay at the cottage. Things appeared to reach an uncanny climax when he discovered the clear imprint of a claw-like hand on a dusty table one morning, but this was nothing compared with what was about to happen.

A local man – a complete sceptic in regards to ghost stories – was so intrigued by the house's growing reputation that he elected to spend the night at the cottage, and it was he who saw a spectre first. The witness and his wife were staying in Mr Davison's room; Mr Davison was asleep in the attic room above them, and a female guest was in an adjoining room. The next morning the sceptical chap commented to the home owner that, 'I'm not laughing at ghosts anymore … I saw one last night.'

According to the man, a small woman holding a tumbler had appeared in the room. So spooked was the witness by the sudden appearance of the figure that he threw one of his shoes at it. The shoe went straight through her! The figure walked slowly towards the wall and then went straight through it. Although the wife of the witness did not see the figure, she told Ian that she had sensed a very oppressive atmosphere and was 100 per cent sure that her husband had not been dreaming. Just a few days later Mr Davison saw the wraith of the woman himself – a forlorn spectre that appeared to him at 4 p.m. The figure was wandering around by the old fireplace and seemed to be looking for something. Her expression was sombre. The woman then disappeared into the wall. After this encounter, Ian would go on to have several more sightings of the miserable-looking old woman.

However, she was not the only spirit in the house: one of the more disturbing apparitions that appeared to Ian was that of a heavily built man who emerged from out of the wall of the large room downstairs. The figure would float to the centre of the room and then stop, turn around and glide back into the area of the open fire. Mr Davison recorded that every time the figure appeared, something weird would happen shortly after. One night, Ian – who had a friend and their dog staying – woke to the sounds of the dog scratching on his bedroom door. When Ian got to his feet he noticed that the bed, and his body, was drenched in sweat. The atmosphere in the room was uncanny – it was as hot as a sauna. Ian, alarmed, thought the house (or a part of it) was on fire, but then he saw a figure materialise in the vicinity of the bedroom door. Ian described the male ghost as 'the foulest-looking man', a ghastly figure dressed in odd, multi-coloured clothes, with a hideous smirk and imposing features. The figure seemed to leer at Ian and then the apparition laughed. Ian was so petrified that he couldn't look at the phantom anymore and turned away, but when he was brave enough to look back he noticed that the figure was losing its shape, became less defined. Eventually the figure seemed to dissipate.

The lady who was staying in the house - who left the next day – reported that she'd been so disturbed by the weird atmosphere of the place at night that she had stayed up, shivering with fear, waiting for the dawn. On another occasion Mr Davison, accompanied by a friend named Bill, decided to conduct a mini ghost-hunt in the house. They didn't find anything outside, but as they came back to the house they described hearing the place 'moan'. It was at this point that several psychic mediums were contacted, in the hope that they could either move the spirits on or at least find out who, or what, haunted the cottage. A Denis Conan Doyle told Ian that the bizarre heat waves that had been soaking the house in moisture were possibly the product of some malevolent manifestation, and it was suggested to Ian that he call in a chap named Ronald Kaulback, a psychic investigator. The next day Conan Doyle, accompanied by Ronald Kaulback and Kaulback's brother, Adrian, visited the cottage. As soon as they entered the large room Ronald sensed a presence and found himself gasping for air. At the same time both Conan Doyle and Davison claimed to have seen a fleeting shadow. The next morning Denis and Adrian had to leave the building, due to commitments elsewhere, but Ronald stayed on and it was during this period when the ghosts of the house seemed to manifest more regularly. According to author Peter Underwood, 'There now appeared to be at least three ghosts: the little old woman in grey; the foul and fearsome male figure and another man who was short and thickly built and very ugly but his appearance never caused Davison any feelings of repulsion.'

There were also occasional encounters with a spectral cat and the sound of wings flapping. One spirit medium told Mr Davison that the spirits of the house may well have been 'negative forms' which were the result of some type of black magic that may have taken place not so long ago. Small bones – believed to have come from a dead baby – were found under the floorboards of the house alongside odd markings, and everything the visiting medium suggested seemed to make sense to Ian.

Research conducted by Ian led him to believe that a black magician – named Tarver – had been practising his unholy rituals in the house and that he had formed some type of cult. Legend went further, saying that people – often young women – had been sacrificed in the house. One man who was bewitched by Tarver's imposing stature and esoteric powers was a man

named Hunter. Although Hunter was not a bad person, once he fell under the spell of Tarver he became his right-hand man. On one occasion, Hunter accidentally witnessed Tarver murdering his mistress. According to Underwood, the mistress's baby had been murdered by Tarver as a sacrificial act. She spent most of her days roaming the house looking for her dead child until she too was murdered. Tarver was so enraged when he realised that what his right-hand man had seen that he killed him too. Underwood concludes that Hunter's body was buried somewhere in the grounds of the property but 'this murder of a member of the coven roused the remainder of the circle to action and eventually Tarver was hanged from a beam in the big room.'

After these horrible events, the cottage stood empty for some thirty odd years, but the negative energy had clearly soaked into the walls of the house, only to be replayed when Ian had unknowingly disturbed their dormancy. One evening Ian had a terrible encounter with the ghost of Tarver. The figure appeared to Ian, at a distance of just 3ft away, near to the bathroom door. However, Ian, despite his fear, refused to back down and challenged the despicable wraith, stating that it was his house and that the spectre should move on from this plateau. With that the ghost of Tarver seemed, for the most part, to exit the realm of the living and pass on. This incredible incident seemed to have had an amazing effect on the other ghosts. Shortly afterwards, Ian had an encounter with the ghostly woman, and noted that she seemed relieved of her torment.

In fact, the woman smiled at him, raised her arms as if to bid farewell and vanished, never to be seen again. A few nights later Ian was lying in bed, wide awake, when he saw the ghost of Hunter standing by his bed. Ian was not afraid of the spirit – in fact, it looked rather forlorn. He addressed the spectre, asking if he could help it in any way move on to the other side. The ghost then bent over Ian, the face of the wraith almost touching his own. Ian tried to speak with the ghost but got no response from the tired-looking man. It hovered over him. Then, at last, after about twenty minutes, the phantom faded.

The next day a spiritualist stayed. During her first night she had a supernatural encounter whilst sleeping in the room that adjoined Ian's. She was awakened in the night by a mist that seemed to rise up from the foot of the bed. Then she saw the ghost of a man walking towards the bed from the right-hand side of the room. The figure came close. Though she was terrified, the witness did not scream; instead, she sensed that the spectre needed to find its way out to the light. The ghost reached out a hand and the woman held it tight. A sound of purring and flapping seemed to come from a corner of the room; the ghostly figure looked in that direction, and then vanished into thin air. The medium was overcome with a weird tingling sensation and noticed that the room was bathed in a peculiar light. The spectre – believed to be that of Hunter – was never seen at the cottage again.

During the early 1980s the cottage's new owners reported to Peter Underwood only the occasional, and vague, sighting of a fleeting figure, but nothing of malevolence. One such ghost story was attached to the old barn and concerned a gardener who claimed to have seen a ghostly figure go into the building. Rumour had it that many years ago a man hanged himself in the barn.

And so it seems that that it is now a house of tranquillity, finally rid of its negative energy – or is it?

Southborough

SOUTHBOROUGH lies to the north of Tunbridge Wells. The name is said to derive from the Norman Conquest, when, alongside three other boroughs, it came within the lands of Tonbridge Castle. Southborough was 'the South Borough'. The fossilized remains of an iguanodon – dating back 125 million years – were discovered at High Brooms clay pit in 1933.

Broomhill Road Strangeness

Tales of phantom horsemen are often best suited to dark and stormy nights, when rain batters the tarmac, thunder reverberates around the black sky and lightning forks spear from the heavens. Many years ago a local man walking on a wooded pathway in the vicinity of Broomhill Road got the shock of his life when a headless horseman, mounted on a spectral horse, came charging through the undergrowth. Legend has it that the ghostly horseman belonged to Cromwell's army who, during the time of the civil war, were said to have occupied the area. No one knows why the horseman is short of a head – the usual thing in such cases – but folklore often suggests that such spectres were decapitated in battle. If so, then this unfortunate apparition may well have succumbed to the blade of a Royalist.

Broomhill Road has another apparition. A man dressed in grey has been reported on the stretch of road by motorists, who often brake to avoid him – only to see him glide through their vehicle. Motorists brave enough to stop and investigate find there

A hideous headless horseman was observed at Broomhill Road. (Illustration by Simon Wyatt)

is no trace of a body. There is a possibility that this sullen wraith is the same man who once occupied a cottage that used to sit on the road many decades ago. A Tonbridge couple named Mr and Mrs Gearing had a peculiar encounter with the Broomhill Road spectre one night whilst driving home from their friend's house. The figure appeared on the verge by the side of the road. As the vehicle approached, both witnesses noted how close he was – surely he would be hit? However, when the car braked, hard, and the couple got out to investigate, they found that there was no sign of the mystery man.

The Willies at Winton Lodge!

According to Peter Underwood's *Ghosts of Kent*, 'Some years ago, when the sixteenth-century house known as Winton Lodge was occupied by Mr and Mrs H. Lloyd, they believed the property was haunted by the ghost of Queen Caroline.' Caroline had been the Queen consort of King George IV from the beginning of 1820 until her death a year later. Queen Caroline was rumoured to have stayed at Winton Lodge with her daughter, Princess Charlotte, during the late 1700s. Maybe her spectre still roams the building? Mrs Lloyd reported seeing a female spectre one afternoon as she approached the house. Standing in the vicinity of the side door was a woman dressed in the sort of old-fashioned dress one might see at a fancy-dress ball. Being polite, Mrs Lloyd said 'Good afternoon' to the woman – who vanished on the spot!

According to Peter, the Lloyds experienced many strange occurrences during their long stay at the house. In 1948 a local newspaper gave the house the title 'most haunted' in Southborough. Most of the activity seems rather vague: lights flickering on and off, and ghostly footsteps heard throughout the building. The only unnerving bout of strangeness to occur took place one night when the couple were in bed: they heard a bedstead in another room begin to shake. On occasion visitors who stayed at the house reported a strange atmosphere, to the extent that they sometimes refused to stay again. The pet dog belonging to Mr and Mrs Lloyd refused to go into some of the rooms of the house. One area in which the dog seemed particularly spooked was in the same doorway that the woman in the white dress had been seen.

More Terrors from the Town

Ghostly Guardians

Author and ghost investigator Andrew MacKenzie speaks of a Tunbridge Wells phantom in his book *Apparitions and Ghosts*. He was contacted by a woman who told him the following story:

> In 1940, at the height of the Battle of Britain, bombs were dropped on Tunbridge Wells and the Calverley Park Pavilion was set alight. A flare fell on our maisonette nearby. It seemed as though a good part of Tunbridge Wells was on fire. I went on to the top floor garden roof and held a ladder for a warden to climb on to the top roof and put it (the flare) out. I felt very frightened. Then suddenly I saw my father standing near smiling at me. Then just as suddenly he was no longer there. It was most vivid. My father had died a few years previously. He was a very kind man and I felt quite comforted.

Another case from the files of MacKenzie is mentioned in John and Anne Spencer's volume *The Encyclopaedia of Ghosts and Spirits*. In 1951, a man named Robert Hughes was asleep in his Tunbridge Wells home, with his young son Malcolm at his side. In the next room slept Robert's wife and Malcolm's older brother, Anthony. During the early hours Mr Hughes awoke and saw a figure of a woman leaning over the bed and looking at Malcolm. The child did not stir from his slumber. Mr Hughes reported that the woman was approximately 5ft 5in tall, had greyish hair tied in a bun and wore a green and brown, heavy-looking dress with pleats. The figure slowly drifted across the room and headed into the other bedroom before fading. Mr Hughes told his wife about the ghost and she suggested that it might have been the spirit of a woman named Ada Phillips, who used to reside at the property. When Ada was alive it was her wish to adopt a child with her husband, but the night before the child was to arrive, Ada suddenly passed away. 'Over the next twenty years,' he concludes, 'Mr Hughes saw the apparition four times.' Maybe the ghost of Mrs Phillips was looking over the family, particularly the boy, protecting them?

Time Slip

One Tunbridge story involves a local woman who had a very strange shopping trip. Stories of ghosts and the like are reported at a regular rate, but one element of the supernatural that occurs more sporadically is a time slip. Can people, accidentally, travel back in time? Many may scoff at the thought, but consider the following incident, which took place on 18 June 1968.

The woman was on a visit to Tunbridge Wells with her husband. The pair decided to shop separately and meet up later. The wife decided to visit a supermarket on the Calverley Road. When she entered the shop, at No. 32, via an archway, things seemed somehow odd – suddenly there was a café which she'd never seen before, filled with people; two women inside were wearing long, old-fashioned dresses. Strangely, there appeared to be no sound coming from the people, even though they were clearly chatting away. Maybe the café had been recently built, she thought – though the decor seemed to suggest otherwise. However, the woman thought nothing else of it; she left the area and met up with her husband but didn't mention the slightly odd experience. However, on another visit to the supermarket the lady decided to take her husband with her to the café. When the couple searched the area they could find no trace of it. They soon learned that the Kosmos Kinema had once stood on the site (it had shut down in 1960), and had in fact housed a café. The café had been removed, and yet the woman would swear that she had visited it. The café area had once belonged to the Constitutional Club, where members would congregate in the bar area for refreshments. Somehow the witness had managed to either step back into another time, or the ghosts of the past – including the building – had made themselves known to her.

The Winged Monster

Some supernatural stories defy belief. The following tale is one of those unique cases. On 19 October 2006, a Tunbridge Wells resident named Jacki had an absurd encounter with a flying anomaly as she looked out of her bedroom window. She had been woken up in the dead of night by a horrendous screeching noise. Gazing out into the night she saw the tail end of

A sinister winged, supernatural creature has been sighted in Tunbridge Wells.

a bizarre creature zoom by. Whilst it could be argued that the witness had simply seen a bird, or even a bat, flitting by the window, this had in fact been the third time Jacki had witnessed the strange creature – as a four-year old girl, she'd named it the 'bat-winged monkey-bird'.

Her first sighting of the entity took place in 1969, while she was sitting in the back of her parent's car on the way home from a relative's house in London. About half an hour into the journey, as they were travelling on a dark, tree-lined road, Jacki heard a terrible screeching noise. Her parents didn't seem to hear the noise – maybe because they'd been busy chatting away in the front of the car? However, Jacki looked out to see what was making the noise – and saw a horror. As she looked out of the back window of the vehicle, she saw a monster which had the wings of a bat, the face of a monkey and a parrot-like beak. It was about 3ft tall.

Her second sighting of the 'bat-winged monkey-bird' took place when she was eleven. Again, she'd looked out of the back window of the car whilst travelling through Robertsbridge, in East Sussex.

Jacki reported her trio of terrifying sightings in the January 2008 issue of the now defunct *Beyond* magazine, and was quite adamant that what she had seen was not a normal animal. Had this monstrous spectre somehow been attached to her psyche, as is the case with some supernatural manifestations? Or had this spectre haunted a vast area for many years? Perhaps the 'bat-winged monkey-bird' is still out there, waiting for a certain type of person to make it manifest?

Woodbury Park Road – ghostly cries have been heard in the area.

Woodbury Park Road

During the middle of the nineteenth century an orphanage used to stand on this road. Tragically, the building succumbed to a raging fire and many of the children within were burned alive. As the building burned, a member of staff gathered them all into one room. When the children were packed in, like sardines, the staff member asked them all to sing; realising, perhaps, that there was no hope for them as the flames lapped at the door. As the fire roared and smoked spilled through the cracks, the children's voices rose high above the crackles until they perished. Some say that on certain nights of the year those young voices can still be heard above the moans of the wind.

Rumour also has it that a woman in a grey, Victorian-style dress has been seen in the vicinity. Could this be the teacher who herded the children into the room?

The Most Haunted Pub in Tunbridge Wells?

Tunbridge Wells is littered with haunted pubs – or so they say. It depends on who you speak to. A disbelieving landlord of an old creaky pub may not know the first thing about the resident spectre, and yet one of the cleaners or a member of the bar staff may have seen more than just the sprits behind the bar!

The Compasses public house (formerly known as The Compasses and Horseshoes and also The Three Compasses), situated at No. 45 Little Mount Sion, has been described as the oldest pub in Tunbridge Wells (although The Grove Tavern also lays claim to this title) and also the most haunted. The building seems to have a handful of ghostly tales attached to it, one concerning a little girl who – according to legend – was murdered many years ago. Her spirit, as well as the ghost of her killer, is said to haunt the premises. In fact, the ghostly activity was rumoured to have reached such

severe levels a few years ago that an exorcist was called in. One member of staff, a chap named Pete, mentioned that he'd seen a spectre of a dark-haired woman in a white smock walk by a door. Other witnesses describe fleeting shadows, inexplicable gusts of wind and sudden cold spots.

A team of investigators by the name of Soul Searchers Kent, a group comprising various psychic mediums, was formed in 2004 by Susie Higgins. A few years ago they were invited to investigate The Compasses after receiving a call from the landlord about the high levels of paranormal activity. Susie wrote in her location report:

> To us it had become quite clear that the pub had a known history for specific

The Compasses – the most haunted pub in Tunbridge Wells?

hauntings, as the owners had subsequently found out when they moved in. Staff had encountered whispers in their ears and a presence elsewhere moving in close by them. The daughter had been told by a male spirit to harm herself. A spirit female child had latched onto her and made herself present in and outside of the pub. After interviewing the couple, we went upstairs to take base readings, photograph key areas and set up the voice recorder. I always like to lock off an area and keep the voice recorder running so that I may catch disembodied voices. The energies in certain rooms were breathtaking!

Some of the photographs taken by the team showed the presence of what are called orbs. Susie also commented that she was touched and felt threatened by a strong male presence and a shadow was seen darting from doorway to doorway. An unseen male presence growled – in a northern accent - at the team to 'Get out!' It seems that the male spirit – in the material world – had owned several of the rooms at the pub and rented them out to prostitutes. According to Susie, 'One of the prostitutes (his favourite) had borne his child, a female. He murdered the mother of his child, and in a very poor fashion and in a very hit-and-miss way he brought up the daughter. She was only around seven when she died (falling over the top step and down the stairs to her death).'

The team hoped to communicate with the spirit of the young girl haunting the property. They believed the girl was named Jennifer. The group formed a circle and, in Susie's words, the girl, who was wearing a white dress and holding a comfy doll, 'looked at us and bade us farewell.'

Shortly afterwards the investigators were successful in sending the hostile male spirit on his way. Susie concluded, 'We have not yet spoken to the family since our visit as it was a short while ago but as we have not heard from them we feel things may be for the better.'

The Grove Tavern, which can be found close to The Compasses, is at No. 19 Berkeley Road. This pub has a ghostly male presence called Joshua who, in the past, has been seen to haunt an old passageway that used to lead to a nearby house of ill-repute. According to landlord Steve Baxter, who has run the pub since 2003, there have been no recent sightings of the spectre.

Meanwhile, in his book *They Walk by Night*, Michael Hervey mentions another Tunbridge Wells pub as being haunted – though sadly he does not give the name of the premises. However, he writes, 'In a pub at Tunbridge Wells, the ghosts even pay for their drinks, for mysteriously money continually appears from nowhere. An old woman once gave the innkeeper's wife a coin claiming it would bring her luck. The old lady died … and the mystery coins have been appearing ever since.'

Another haunted pub is the Opera House (now a Wetherspoon's) situated on Mount Pleasant. On Sunday, 10 April 2011, a ghost hunt took place at the Opera House. It's no surprise that such a building attracts ghost-hunters when one considers that it's more than 100 years old. It began life in 1902, and was made into a cinema in 1931 and then, in the 1970s, became a bingo hall. In 1997 the Opera House became a pub.

The Opera House.

The Major's Ghost – a Mystery Within a Mystery

On the 9 November 1905 an atmospheric story appeared in the *Ludington Daily News* under the heading, 'The Major's Ghost'. I reproduce the entire article here to prove that some alleged ghostly tales can, in fact, be solved – even if the truth of the saga is a little weird too.

Legend has it that one of the theatre boxes is haunted. Strangely, the apparitions are not of some long-lost theatregoers but, in fact, those of the builders who constructed the balcony area. Three men were said to have fallen from their scaffolding whilst they were working on the ceiling. Oddly, only two of these builders are said to haunt the balcony area. Maybe, as Christopher Cassidy writes at his anke.blogs.com, these two were friends who often ate their lunch here together?

Thirty miles out of London, and between the villages of Tunbridge Wells and Little Manor, was the property of Sir Hugh Cullom, deceased. He had been a bachelor, and the property had fallen to a relative whose whereabouts were not known. It was only a small landed estate of about fifty acres, and the house had hardly been habitable during the last five years of the owner's life. Left without a caretaker, another five years made it little better than a ruin. When grounds are neglected and overgrown and a house goes to decay it does not take long for a rustic population to give it a bad name and connect a ghost with it. It was so in this case. Once a couple of boys reported seeing a man's face at one of the lower windows, but the story passed for what it was worth. Only a few people would have it that the house was haunted, but all seemed to tacitly agree that it was a good place to keep away from.

One day Major Killaine came down from London for a week's fishing and put up at the Sundial. It was not long before the gossips posted him regarding the Cullom house, and what was said seemed to stick in his mind. He said little, but that night after supper he took a walk over the highway toward the house and was gone for three hours. Next day he went to Tunbridge Wells and bought himself a revolver and a box of cartridges, and he was absent again for the next two nights. Parties who recognised him met him near the house and saluted him. After his third visit he was found in the house a corpse. At the inquest, later on, the landlord of the Sundial had an interesting story to tell. He said that when Major Killaine returned from his first expedition he called him into his bedroom and told him that he had entered the grounds and even the house, and, though he was not attacked as others had been, he had reasons for believing that men were hanging about. He proposed to arm himself and solve the mystery and bound the landlord to secrecy. The landlord could not say whether the major visited the place in the daytime or not, but he knew that his second visit at night confirmed the suspicions born on the first. When he went away on the third night he was somewhat excited, saying that he expected to meet with a lively adventure. It was suggested that he take one of the county policemen with him, but this he would not listen to. Whatever it was, he wanted to meet it single-handed.

It was a dark and rainy night in September when the major set forth on his trip, and he took with him candle and matches and a flask of wine. He had not returned at 11 o'clock, when the house was closed and the host went to bed. Some uneasiness was felt next day when he did not appear, and after another twelve hours the landlord went to the legal authorities. For a day they refused to interfere, but when officers finally went to inspect the house they found the major lying stiff and dead in the lower hall. It was at first believed that murder had been done, but when the doctors came to examine the dead man not a mark of violence could be found on him. A post-mortem revealed the fact that he had died of heart failure. The house was searched from top to bottom, and, though there were traces of human behaviour having been around of late, there were no other discoveries.

Here was a mystery within a mystery. It was the opinion of the country doctors and the officers of the law that the major had overexerted himself in walking the 2 miles after a hearty supper, and but for his brother in London that would have been the verdict of the coroner's jury and the end of the case. As soon as the brother came down, however, he sent for detectives and insisted on a thorough probing. The sleuths were at work for three months, and it was while they were still at work on the case that they made the arrest of a noted burglar. The man was picked up almost by accident; and it turned out that he held the key to the mystery. Some weeks previous to the major's coming a country bank had been robbed of a large sum in gold by two men. They stole a horse and buggy to carry their plunder away, and the police were baffled for a clew [sic]. It seems that they drove to the house and secreted their plunder in the cellar and hid themselves in an upper room. They were aware of the major's first and second visits and were prepared for his third. With phosphorous they drew a skeleton on the unpapered wall of the hall and covered it over with a blanket. When the major entered the house and before he had struck a light the blanket was removed and dismal groaning indulged in to heighten the effect. The soldier had proved his bravery on many a field, but the sight and noises came to him with such a sudden shock that he fell back dead.

The gold was still in the cellar, waiting for the hue and cry to subside, but it was taken out that night and buried on the grounds, and the men separated. The arrest of one bought about the arrest of the other, and every dollar of the plunder was restored to the bank. But for the major's curiosity the men might have eventually got away with the spoils, but he would not have met the end he did.

Assembly Hall Anomalies

Assembly Hall, on Crescent Road.

The Tunbridge Wells Assembly Hall, situated on Crescent Road, opened in 1939. Over the years it has put on a number of shows, all to the joy of the 1,000 or so people who filled the seats. In fact, the variety of performers who set foot on the stage each year currently attracts around 150,000 people. It could also be said that the Assembly Hall has attracted a few ghosts!

On 4 April 1964 a man died in the basement when he fell into a vat of oil. The spectre is often blamed for the sudden drop in temperature, the slamming of doors and the light switches which are turned on and off. Members of staff have reported all manner of peculiar bumps – or perhaps, as the nights draw in, minds run wild. Even so, theatre director Brian McAteer reported that a white lady has been seen gliding across the circle. In some cases of phantom females, witnesses note a sweet odour, such as lavender, but in the case of this apparition there seems to be a terrible stench attached to its appearance.

Mr McAteer reported on the 'So Tunbridge Wells' website that he'd had a couple of eerie experiences. One night, whilst working alone, he heard footsteps on the balcony situated behind his office. When he went to investigate he found no one there. The theatre has another intriguing legend attached to a noose which hangs from a grid above the stage. In 1951 an actor died on stage, and ever since his death the noose has remained – but should it be removed then that person will suffer a terrible accident, or even death.

So there you have it – a curious collection of ghostly tales and weird legends from the Tunbridge Wells District. Now that the ghost train has come to a halt, it's up to you whether you want to get off!

It's the shapeless entity at the foot of the
  bed
A poltergeist, night terror and spirit of the
  undead.
Beyond wildest dreams and from
  nightmares cast,
The power of the ghost story – a menace
  built to last.

Bibliography and Sources

And then it was gone, in the blink of an eye,
I wish I'd got the chance to ask it who and why!

Books

Alexander, Marc, *Haunted Houses You May Visit* (Sphere, 1982)

Arnold, Neil, *Mystery Animals of the British Isles: Kent* (CFZ Press, 2009)

Arnold, Neil, *Paranormal Kent* (The History Press, 2010)

Butcher, Josephine, *I Was Born on the Pantiles* (Turney Publications, 1990)

Canning, John ed., *50 Great Horror Stories* (Souvenir Press, 1971)

Campbell, Mary, *A Walk in Old Tunbridge Wells* (privately published)

Conan Doyle, Sir Arthur, *The Edge of the Unknown* (J. Murray, 1930)

Dixon, G.M., *Folktales of Kent* (Minimax, 1984)

Forman, Joan, *The Haunted South,* (Jarrold, 1978)

Green, Andrew, *Haunted Kent Today* (S.B. Publications, 1999)

——— *Phantom Ladies* (Bailey Brothers & Swinfen Ltd, 1977)

Haining, Peter ed., *True Hauntings* (Robinson, 2008)

Hapgood, Sarah, *The World's Greatest Ghost & Poltergeist Stories* (Foulsham, 1994)

Harper, Charles G., *Haunted Houses* (Senate, 1994)

Harries, John, *The Ghost Hunter's Road Book* (Muller, 1968)

Hervey, Michael, *They Walk By Night* (Ace, 1968)

Johnson, W.H., *Kent Stories of the Supernatural* (Countryside Books, 2000)

Long, Roger, *Haunted Inns Of Kent* (S.B. Publications, 2005)

Ludlum, Harry, *Ghosts Among Us* (Janus, 1994)

MacKenzie, Andrew, *Apparitions & Ghosts* (Arthur Barker, 1971)

Matthews, Rupert, *Haunted Places Of Kent* (Countryside, 2004)

Paine, Brian ed., *Unexplained Kent* (Breedon, 1997)

Playfair, Guy Lyon, *The Haunted Pub Guide* (Javelin, 1985)